What's LUST Got to do with it?

7 Steps to Breaking the Bondage of Your Past

By

Dr. Deb Gold

ISBN-13: 978-1916787841 Dr. Deb Gold
(Manning the Gate Publishing LLC)

What's LUST Got to do with it? Copyright © 2023
by Dr. Deborah Wiley Gold

All rights reserved.

The information in this book is based on the author's knowledge, research, education, experience, and opinions. The theology, exegesis, and hermeneutics described in this book are the author's opinions and theories. Your opinions may differ.

This work depicts actual events in the life of the author as truthfully as recollection permits and/or can be verified by research. Occasionally, dialogue consistent with the character or nature of the person speaking has been supplemented. All persons within are actual individuals; there are no composite characters. The names of some individuals have been changed to respect their privacy.

Copyright © 2023 Dr. Deborah Wiley Gold. All rights are reserved, including the right to reproduce this book or portions thereof. No part of this book may be reproduced in any form without the author's express written permission.

Editor – Jo Fouts Zausch

Narrator – Lynn Marie Brunk

Front Cover by Aimee Brooke Schindler

Endorsements

This book by Dr. Deb Gold is engagingly written, yet sound in its advice, very practical, and personal.

We see yet again the impact of generations of trauma, while also being given a path to healing and freedom from its entanglement.

As a therapist working with those who have suffered trauma, I can attest to the truth of what Dr. Gold writes and the importance of following the 7 steps Dr. Gold outlines in order to achieve true healing and move beyond trauma to a life of joy and fulfillment.

Inspiring story that provides hope and a path to healing beyond where traditional psychotherapy ends.

Rachele L. Floyd, Psy.D.
Clinical Psychologist, Oklahoma
St. Dymphna Psychological Services, PLLC

Dr. Gold has written a gut wrenchingly honest book that will allow so many traumatized people to heal. By telling her story from such an honest approach, she exhibited great courage. Because of her compassion to help people she took the risk of opening up, and I am sure that her book will free many traumatized people that are frozen in unforgiveness. My prayer is that every person that needs to learn about how to forgive and the power it releases will read this book. Thank you for having the courage to write this book with such clarity and honesty. Dr. Gold gives hope for the wounded that there is life after pain and trauma.

Mark M Sneed, PhD Director of Oklahoma Christian Counseling Center

"What's Lust Got to Do with It?" is not just a book; it is an invitation to embark on a transformative journey of healing and wholeness. Dr. Gold's compassionate and nonjudgmental tone reassures readers that there is hope and redemption even in the midst of their deepest pain. She reminds us that true healing can only come through surrendering our brokenness to God and allowing Him to work in us. Whether you are a survivor of trauma, a counselor, or a concerned individual wanting to support others on their healing journey, this book will provide you with invaluable guidance and wisdom.

Charli M. Brown, MSN
Founder-The Rooted Kafe, Author, Speaker

As Dr. Gold's former Clinical Director and witness to her life the last 25 years of the story that she has shared in this book, I can personally and professionally attest to her capturing the winning formula for victims of trauma and abuse. Any reader, living with, through, or personally dealing with the effects of lust and trauma will find healing and hope. This is a great tool for anybody's tool belt!

Sincerely,

Mark E. Nathanson, Ph.D.
Children's Social Worker
Los Angeles County, Department of Children and family Services

Table of Contents

DEDICATION i
ACKNOWLEDGEMENT ii
ABOUT THE AUTHOR iii
INTRODUCTION 1
CHAPTER ONE: SO IT BEGINS 7
CHAPTER TWO: WHAT'S LUST GOT TO DO 13
CHAPTER THREE: THE PAIN IS THE DOOR TO OPEN PANDORA'S BOX 25
CHAPTER FOUR: PAIN HAS POWER, AND SO DOES JOY .. 31
CHAPTER FIVE: REALIZING THE TRUTH 45
CHAPTER SIX: PAIN REFINES YOU; 51
CHAPTER SEVEN: REALIZING THE POWER OF SELF THROUGH FORGIVENESS 59
CHAPTER EIGHT: WHEN I DON'T RECOGNIZE 71
CHAPTER NINE: HOW IT KEEPS HAPPENING 79
CHAPTER TEN: GENERATIONAL CURSES 85
THE 7 STEPS TO BREAKING THE BONDAGE OF YOUR PAST 101

Dedication

I dedicate this book first and foremost to my Lord, who brought me through every storm, protected me, strengthened me through all my trials, and stood beside me even when I stumbled and turned my back on Him. Yet, He always loved me, forgave me, was patient with me, and still had my back. At my lowest points, He wept with me, and at my pinnacles, He cheered me on. Lord, this book is for you. I hope you use this book to heal all who have been victims or perpetrators of lust in one form or another. Thank you for your love and compassion.

Acknowledgement

A special thanks to my family. My loving husband Stephen, whose encouragement is continuous. My children, Vickie, Greg, and Melissa who, stood by me through the good and bad and never quit believing in me. Vickie is my oldest daughter whom I was pregnant with as I stood on the bridge ready to jump and take her life as well as mine and the children she would have and the children and grandchildren I would have. Vickie wrote chapter 10. She gave her story from her perspective. Vickie, thank you for your honesty and vulnerability.

A special thank you to my editor, Jo Zausch, who inspired me, and Bonnie Manning, who encouraged me.

I also dedicate this book to my dad, who always loved me unconditionally. Mom, many people have been healed through your pain. I wish you were here to see it. I love you.

About the Author

Dr. Deborah Gold is an author and motivational empowerment coach in the field of Trauma recovery. She has been a practicing behavioral therapist since 1990. She received her Ph.D. in Psychology in 1999. In addition, Dr. Deb also earned a bachelor's degree in theology. She is a Bible teacher and a sought-after national conference speaker. Her wit and humor have given her an edge in driving home the difficult truths with the ability to laugh at herself while providing the opportunity for others to recover and heal. Her message is one of redemption and hope.

Deborah's Passion is to help women and young people recover from the trauma of sexual, emotional, spiritual, and physical abuse. She has helped thousands in her career to recover and lead happy and productive lives.

INTRODUCTION

My name is Deborah Gold. I have a Ph.D. in psychology and am the founder and Executive Director of two non-profit organizations. I have also been a wife and a mother who sat at home alone with three children and wondered if their alcoholic father would come home with any money for rent or food after drinking or gambling all week.

At fifteen years old, I stood on a bridge, pregnant and alone, prepared to jump into the murky waters below to kill myself and my unborn child. After overcoming and healing from these desperate situations, my heart was encouraged to co-found an organization that serves troubled youth and their families. Our mission with this organization is to help youth in trouble like I had been as a teenager. We long to rescue them from themselves and to help turn their lives around. The organization was named UCAN and was founded in 1990. I have established another non-profit, a women's organization, WOMEN of MERIT Ministries, whose mission is to assist women in overcoming the pain of both physical and emotional abuse. I, too, have felt such pain. I desire to help them recover, reestablish themselves, and bring them the hope of becoming whole again.

I have experienced much pain in my lifetime, and I have learned much from it. On this journey, I have also been a senior pastor of a congregation. My husband, at the time, was the co-pastor with me. He left the ministry and me, his wife, to pursue younger women and a different lifestyle even though I was ten years younger than him.

So, from all these life-altering experiences, I have also felt the call to help others in their pain. How I survived all of this is still a puzzle to me when I look back, except for the strength I was given, which I am sure came from somewhere beyond my strength. I am called to help others not because I believe I am better or brighter than others but because I have found what I consider are the keys to restoration and wholeness, no matter how bad things are. This is my story of overcoming the darkest hours of my life.

I wanted to write this book because I believe that as you read this, you will gain the faith to understand nothing is impossible. I have spent countless years struggling to make sense of this thing called life. I have gone from being a troubled young girl: a victim of childhood trauma and molestation, a teenage runaway, and homeless living in a period of poverty and abuse. I have had the guilt and failure of two marriages and divorces and was even suicidal at one point. I went from being homeless to completing a Ph.D. I would have never believed this could be possible. Between the pages of this book, you will see the many times I felt like giving up. I wanted to quit, but I somehow found the strength that kept me moving forward and never turning back. There is power in the forward motion. No matter how hard it is, keep going and keep moving forward.

I found the power that comes with true faith. True faith is faith that overcomes. It is the faith of going and doing, not looking back, and never giving up. I found strength in gratitude no matter how doubtful I was or how terrible it looked. I found the rainbow in the darkest clouds because of my faith. When my little brother Danny and I would sneak into bed with each other because we were scared, he would always ask me to sing the song *"Somewhere Over the Rainbow"* before we went to sleep. I didn't know then that I would constantly search for the rainbow in the storms I would face. I wasn't even aware these types of storms could or would ever exist in our lives when we were so young.

I am hopeful this book will bring you the answers you are looking for. No matter how many people have been willing to throw you away, you are worth saving. You are precious in the eyes of God. It doesn't matter how you see yourself. Your life, despite mistakes, has significance. I have never seen myself as extraordinary. Quite the opposite, I have always felt very ordinary.

If you had asked the 14-year-old me, I would have told you this life isn't worth the effort. But I have found that God loves ordinary people. The men who failed in the Bible, the emotionally crippled, the woman at the well who lived in sin, these sins were all mine also.

I felt a call to write this book, not because I am unique in any way. I found the greatest joy and peace after what looked like the most impossible situations because those were the times I relied on God and not myself. I have felt like nothing was going to work for me. You will see how a silly, and careless kid can make it, how a woman who made so many wrong decisions could overcome almost anything thrown at her. I want you to see the rainbow shining just ahead of your storm. If I can overcome it, anyone can. I hope you know you don't have to be special or remarkable. As you will see, my life was a big fat mess with bad decisions and wrong behavior, But not beyond the power and love of God! This book will help you know that you don't have to be the strongest or the smartest to be the best you can be. To find true joy is to let go and keep moving. I want you to see what can happen if you let go and trust God.

The Bible tells a story about a potter working with broken pottery. The vessel spins round and round, much as I have felt, my life has felt, but the beauty comes to this pottery by the potter's hands. Those hands are God's hands. His specialty? He loves putting the broken pieces back together. He is molding us and shaping us. But the kicker?

God is using our brokenness to do the healing in us and others. The beauty lies in our brokenness. This book shows the contrast between submitting to God's healing hand and stubbornly refusing. I want you to see the psychological impact you pass on to future generations when you give up – not only psychologically but spiritually and, dare I say, even economically and socially.

This book will help you understand how lust and generational curses are passed on from one generation to the next, even if it is not your lust but someone else's. My gut tells me you bought this book because somehow lust has damaged your heart and life. You may struggle with letting go and finding healing and restoration paths. You will find the answers and steps outlined in this book.

There is an election going on in your life right now. It is a primary election that you will win. Your adversary, the Devil, is running against you. Yet he will be defeated. And a joyful and triumphant life is the outcome you will receive from this ballot box and election. Guess who casts the deciding vote. It is you! No one else's vote counts except for God's! Did you know that the one vote that matters most has already been cast? God's vote for you was already counted! It was cast the day you were conceived; His vote was in. You have been ahead in the polls since before you were born.

He already knew the mistakes and challenges that you would face to be an overcomer in your life. This book is your election strategy to heal and restore your life to a triumphant victory.

The fight for your healing is not defensive. It is an offensive battle to regain what was taken from you.

In this book, I am outlining seven strategies to heal from sexual, emotional, and spiritual abuse. Now is the time. *What's Lust Got to*

Do With It? Everything!

If you or your spouse were addicted to pornography, you need healing. Suppose you were molested or betrayed by adultery, whether it was by physical adultery or by cyberporn. Betrayal is betrayal, and it all feels the same. If similar experiences are yours, it is imperative that you are healed. God's desire and mine for your life is complete restoration. What does that mean? What does complete restoration even look like? Restoration means to be restored to your original condition before so many toxic attacks were mounted against you. It is like restoring an antique automobile. The goal is to return it to its original condition. Restoration in your life means a clean slate. To truly be your authentic self before years of abuse caused you to doubt your worthiness. You may even carry shame that is not yours, yet it haunts you. It was, by design, meant to paralyze you and keep you from the ability to live free and be free. I have been where you are standing. I have fought what you are fighting. Now is the time to learn the keys to obtaining your complete healing.

CHAPTER ONE
SO IT BEGINS

September 30, 2009, was the beginning of my life in many ways. I stood at the cemetery where I buried my mother. I went to the cemetery that day to see my mother's grave, pray, and contemplate where I was at in my life. While I stood looking at my mother's grave, I received a call from a client. I explained to him where I was, and that I was unavailable. This person sounded desperate to talk to someone, so I said he could meet me there. I had stayed there to see this person because I thought I was going to help him heal. I was there (I thought) as a superhero to save the day. It seemed rather bizarre to meet someone at a cemetery. I have never met with anyone at a cemetery before or since then.

On top of the strange surroundings for a counseling session, I was about to get a big surprise! Thank God, my Heavenly Father, who cares so much that He doesn't mind upsetting the apple cart to make sure and show me the truth. Things I had never considered before smacked me right in the face. After all, who could ever help me? I was there to help everyone else. I had spent a significant part of my adult life smiling outside yet hurting internally in silence, always wondering does anyone see me, the real me. I mean the true me, the little girl inside that is crying out for acceptance. Look at me! Do you really see me? I am a good person, and I can be funny who can resist that? I can be charming, and I'll be your friend. Then, you might think I am worthy enough for you to love me. I will even bribe you by trying to help you, perhaps even taking care of you in some way, or I could make you laugh and help you forget. Somehow, I always seemed to get hurt and ended up disappointed time and time again. It felt as if pure, true happiness was for everyone else but not me. Why could I never find it? Of course, I did have moments of pure joy and happiness. Inside, though, I usually felt plagued by performance, never quite good enough. In my mind, I believed I must always look perfect and act perfect, or who could ever love me? No one has yet. What a burden I was carrying. I had no idea or realization that I was even carrying this weight. I knew God loved me unconditionally, but I never felt worthy of His or other people's love unless I performed well.

Things were not going as I had expected. I thought emotional healing was a part of my calling. It was my life work, after all, to be about the business of rescuing everyone else, restoring healing, and making people laugh again, love again, trust again – helping others heal and recover. Helping them to understand their problems and mistakes, all the while burying my own. Hmmm, maybe a cemetery was appropriate (God has such a sense of humor). Who would ever think life could begin in a graveyard? But I now believe that is what happened to me. Because of this encounter, destiny and true freedom had opened for me. Although I was not aware of it yet.

Jesus said in John 8:32, NKJV: "And you shall **know** the truth, and the truth will make you free." While in fact, true freedom comes in the "knowing," and the understanding of knowledge. You see, I had known that I had real pain in my life and that in so many areas I still needed healing. True knowing means clear understanding, and God began to take me on a journey, and I am inviting you to join me. I believe true healing and deliverance will unfold for you as it has for me in the pages of this book. Our Father is about to set you free forever. He is about to turn all your suffering and pain into a gain for you and in everyone's life you touch.

As I stood that day in the cemetery, I looked curiously into the eyes of this man, a client, as he began to share his story with me. He started with tears, saying that I had no clue what it was like to be driven by a generational curse like lust. No one, especially someone like me, could know or understand the depth of pain unless they had experienced it themselves. Really Mr.?? I thought to myself. I saw the pain in his eyes but was not sure if I did understand. Honestly, I felt numb at that moment despite his tears and the obvious pain he was feeling. I was not sure I even wanted to understand. I honestly didn't care. There were so many reasons for my lack of compassion. I never really wanted to hear again from another man giving me the excuses for why he was unfaithful and how sorry he was for it. My second husband of nearly 25 years had recently left me for another woman, and so my compassion tank at this point was below empty. As a country song says, *"My Give a Damn was Busted."* But, of course, I listened, trying to pretend a measure of compassion. But all I truly felt was disdain, and I felt repulsed by his confession.

In my mind, as my client and I walked over to my mother's grave to pray, he was still trying to make me feel sorry for him. I suppose I felt like he needed to find someone who cared. That wasn't even possible for me because my heart was so hardened by this time.

As I stood over my mother's grave, I prayed silently and permitted God to pull out every root of the pain in my heart. Listening to this man, I realized how much healing I still needed. God, I cried out in my heart; I didn't want to be like my poor mother. She went from one bad relationship to another; she was married four times, never finding what she was so desperately searching for. Nothing would ever complete her broken heart. She spent most of her life bitter and angry, often crawling into a bottle to cope and ultimately dying alone, never finding the love she so hungered for again. Please, God, do not let her lot be mine. I realized at that moment that I needed help that was beyond me. I just didn't know where to get it. I was always so sure of myself, at least in what I wanted. I felt this morning so alone and confused. As a professional therapist and pastor, I had to admit that I would tell any woman or man in this situation, "Houston, you have a problem!" Like my mother, the sad truth was that I had made significant mistakes in my life. I had twice chosen men I married who abused me and used me. Because of adultery and alcoholism, and prescription drug addictions, they were both relationships that ended in divorce.

My mother took a lot of her pain and anger out on me when I was young. As I grew up, she projected much of her shame and guilt upon me. I don't blame my mother for any of it. She did not like females very much, and I was one of those creatures, of course. She was a victim too. How could I blame her? I did blame her when I was younger because I couldn't understand why she couldn't love me the way she did my younger brother. Let me explain further. Here I want to tell you my mother's first name was Betty. Her (Betty's) mother's name was Pauline. Now I will explain at least partially their lives to you.

Her mother, my grandmother, Pauline, died when Betty was 11 years old. Betty's Father came to her bedroom on the day of Pauline's funeral. She thought he was there to console her, but instead, he told her he was not her birth father and proceeded to rape her. Can you even imagine being 11 years old, losing your mother, your father, and your innocence all in one day? There was no wonder she became bitter and angry and, yes, even shameful. The shame wasn't hers, yet she carried it all the same. Isn't it odd how one person's lust can transcend generations with its poison and pain? My mother and I never discussed the event because she became furious if I or anyone brought it up. She told me one time about it, so to her, that was enough. I always avoided the topic after that.

As a result of my own experiences, I know the questions young raped or molested girls ask themselves. Did I cause this? What is wrong with me? Why did this happen to me? It had to be my fault somehow. I had asked myself these very questions before. I am sure her stepfather told her he couldn't help himself because she was so pretty. Perpetrators always lay the blame on the victims. That is how they cope with what they have done. I am sure by Betty's behavior that she felt guilt for somehow being responsible for shaming herself and her mother, Pauline. However, nothing could be further from the truth. She may have even disassociated herself from it to cope. Did this really happen? Was it just a horrible dream? A nightmare?

I remember the first night my uncle found his way to my bedroom. I was shocked at his fondling and did not know whether to run or scream. My heart was pounding. I felt like this was wrong but somehow pleasurable. I was so hungry for someone to love me. Was this love? I was so confused. However, I very well remember the shame and guilt I felt. The following few times, he came into my bedroom; I lay awake wondering if the bedroom door would open again and what I would do. Then one night, the unthinkable happened. He penetrated me. I remember jumping up and running across the hall to the bathroom as fast as I could. I began to throw up in the toilet. I just barely made it! My mind was racing like crazy. What am I going to do now? He had actually done it. He completed actual intercourse with me. My body hurt, and I was so sick to my stomach. I remember jumping in the bathtub. I just wanted to wash that night away, but I couldn't, no matter how hard I scrubbed. The humiliation and shame wouldn't go away. There was so much I needed to sort through. I was only thirteen years old. I really didn't have much experience or wisdom to draw from. In fact, that part of my brain wasn't even fully developed yet.

Neurosciences Have taught us the frontal cortex of the brain is not fully developed until somewhere between 25 and 29 years of age. This is the area of our brains where logic and reason and decisions come from. It is no wonder we make very foolish and faulty decisions in our younger years. Not to mention how trauma also affects the process of sound reason. We are not operating with a fully developed or equipped brain.

Although, of course, at the time, I felt very grown up and most capable of sound decisions and good judgement. What would I do? How did this happen? These questions were the most pressing questions in my mind at this moment. I will explore this in the next chapter.

CHAPTER TWO
WHAT'S LUST GOT TO DO WITH IT?

Let me begin this chapter with some information about my early life. I will add more detail later. I ran away from home at 14 years of age. As you read, my uncle, my mother's half-brother, was molesting me. These molestations occurred shortly after my parents' divorce. My molester told me that my parents didn't love me, and I, of course, believed it. He often said to me that I was nothing more than a glorified babysitter for my little brother. This statement was pretty easy for me to believe as my father had moved out, and my mother was working all the time. I did do a lot of babysitting for my brother. Don't get me wrong, I was very close to my brother and loved him very much. However, my emotions were being played like a fiddle, like in the song *"The Devil Went Down to Georgia."* The Lord led me to Florida. So, I left home at 14. How did I leave home? I ran away from home and hitchhiked from Indiana all the way to Miami, Florida. I chose Florida because it had beaches, and I didn't need to take winter clothes with me. I could travel light. I was making adult decisions with the mind of a child. I was operating on pure emotion. I remember the fear of leaving but feeling so unwanted. I thought, what do I have to lose? I might as well live my own life. Nobody cares about me anyway. Do they? I made plans to leave the following day after making my decision to leave home. What was my brilliant plan? I decided to give my brother my Beatles collection of 45s. I swore him to secrecy. He was happy to take my bribe, which sadly only reinforced my conclusion that nobody cared about me, even him. Of course, I did not consider that he was just ten years old and had no idea what he agreed to or that I would be going away for a very long time.

I remember heading out, looking like I was going to school that fateful day. I had my notebook binder and schoolbooks in tow as if I was actually going to school. I caught a bus for the first leg of my journey and found I could go all the way to Kentucky on this bus line. I left my schoolbooks in a phone booth. You know, a phone booth like Clark Kent used to change into Superman instead of a runaway kid – except I was changing from a 14-year-old schoolgirl into a runaway with absolutely no direction. What a little girl I was. As I am looking back in time, it is so easy to see now. At the time, thinking I was grown up, I thought nothing of what might be lying ahead.

I hitchhiked from then on. I usually caught my following rides at truck stops along the way. I only went with truck drivers. The truck drivers I met always seemed so kind and concerned about me traveling like this. I do clearly remember one night in GA. I was waking up from sleeping in a field. I was covered in dew, wet, scared of where to go next, and a little hungry. I looked up and saw a cemetery nearby. I saw a bunch of people standing at a monument. I remember thinking they looked like such a lovely family. I missed being part of a family like that. My heart hurt for what I felt was to be no more. A young couple approached me and asked if I needed help. I must have looked a fright. The family was smiling at me and asked how they might help me. I told them I was hungry. The young man pulled out of his pocket a fifty-dollar bill and handed it to me. I was shocked. I told them I couldn't take this; I had no way to pay it back. I remember he said someday you would find someone who needs help. Just help them. What a prophetic word that turned out to be. I have never forgotten that young couple. In fact, when I have often helped someone, I know can't pay me back, I think of them and how far their fifty-dollar gift has gone by helping this scared, misguided runaway.

I made it to Florida and ended up in Miami Beach. I spent a lot of time in the Jewish area. The shopkeepers were so kind, and funny. I really needed to laugh. They always encouraged me and told me I needed to go back home. I should have listened. But I was too afraid. So many awful things could have happened to me on this journey, but God was with me, protecting me and guiding me along the way.

I ended up with my children's father in Miami. I believed we were so much in love. I had, at last, found the love I desired. I didn't know what an alcoholic was. I was so young. I thought, yeah, he likes to drink and have fun. We slept on the beach, often under bridges. He would leave me to go get temporary work. Most of the time, he would disappear for days. So mostly, I had to fend for myself. I remember collecting bottles I found. In those days, I could turn soda bottles in for cash. I would buy nutritious meals like candy bars and sodas. I could cut a candy bar into small pieces and sometimes make it last for a few days if I had to. I soon found myself fifteen and pregnant – more on this to follow.

Now, let us go back to the cemetery and encounter with the client. I drove away from the graveyard that night, not fully understanding what I had given God permission to do. But I was on my way to a divine encounter with God like nothing I had ever experienced before. At this point, I was feeling some strange confusion and pain deep within my very being. However, I vividly remember a somewhat similar encounter with God when I was 15 years old, alone, and pregnant. The encounter was at night; I stood on a bridge in Miami,

Florida, I planned on taking my life. I was desperate. I was living on the streets, or I would stay in a cheap hotel room when I could earn a few dollars. Sometimes I could get a bunk at a mission, but they asked too many questions for a young runaway girl without parents. My baby's father was around but drunk most of the time and not much help. I had nowhere to go, nowhere to turn. It was only God that kept me safe from harm during that time. But I did not recognize his protection yet. If I went back home, I felt they would take my baby away from me and put me in a juvenile detention center, so what was the point?

That night I was ready to jump into the cold, murky dark waters below and end my life and the life of my unborn child. I remember looking at the river below, trying to get my courage. Then I looked up to the sky and screamed at God. The tears were streaming down my face. Really, God, I shouted. This is it. This is what life is all about? Nothing but hurt and pain? Fear, pain, and what next? I felt so done with this life; it was not worth trying! I know I heard the voice of God that night gently yet firmly say to me: "Step down and back off the bridge. Do not do this; I have more for you than this. The life inside of you is mine, and it is not yours to take."

I didn't know Him very well back then. Sure, I believed in Him and even spoke to Him or yelled at Him in this case, but my relationship with Him was pretty superficial at that point. However, it was undeniable that He knew my child and me. I will never forget that moment as I stepped back from the edge of the bridge, wondering what had just happened, scared out of my mind. I sat there for over an hour, just crying but feeling an incredible warmth and peace. My bones felt like they had turned to butter, and I could not stop shaking, but honestly, at this point, I did not understand why. I did learn from this experience an essential lesson. When you have an encounter like this, listen. Be still. God loves you more than you can fathom. He came to me that night like a real superhero to save my and my baby's lives. I was so misguided to believe that God didn't care because bad things had happened to me. Did he know me? Did He care about this misguided and lost teenager? The God of the universe cared what happened to me. He did! But that was then, and this is now.

On my long drive home in the dark, I began to think about what that man had confessed to me. As I pondered, I began to say to myself, "Thank God that I don't have this kind of problem." That man admitted an addiction to porn and lust that had controlled the entirety of his life. How sad that would be! Suddenly I felt my body begin to shudder and tremble, and I questioned in my mind what in the world was happening to me. Then, at that very moment, I heard this still, small voice deep in my spirit say: "But lust has controlled your entire life." I recognized this as the voice of God deep in my soul. I knew that nothing could have been further from my mind and certainly nothing I would say to myself! I began to tremble even more. I quickly pulled the car to the side of the road; I could not drive any further for fear I was losing control. I knew I was in the middle of something extraordinary happening, a divine encounter that would change my life.

After the shock of what was happening, I immediately became defensive and argumentative with the Lord. What had I just heard? I certainly am not controlled by lust; both of my marriages ended in divorce because of their infidelity, not mine. I almost felt accused or condemned. So, I boldly came to my defense. Oh yeah, God, why did I run away from home at 14 years of age? Because I was being used and abused, molested by my uncle, my mother's half-brother, living with us after my father moved out. I was not quite 13 years old when this started happening. I wasn't molesting anyone! What about that, God? What do you mean my life is controlled by lust? I am the victim here! My mind was hurling thoughts around like a dust devil in the desert sand.

A multitude of whirling thoughts – I had not liked living with my mother after their divorce. I even asked my father if I could stay with him. His response was no because he wanted me to help Mom with my little brother. He said he desired my brother and me to be together. So instead, I ran away because my father wouldn't let me move in with him. I knew he loved me, but I could not tell him why I wanted to move in. I thought He would kill my uncle if he found out and then go to prison for the rest of his life. Why did I believe such a thing? Because my uncle told me that is what would happen if I told anyone. I loved my dad. He was the only one who had ever shown me unconditional love. There was no way I was going to do this to him.

Then how was I supposed to tell my mom? She would never believe me. Even when I won awards at school for accomplishments or anything, I would ask the teacher to give me a note because my mom never thought it was true, even though I was a straight-A student. So how would she believe her 26-year-old half-brother was molesting me? Fat chance. I felt engulfed in a sea of confusion and pain at this point in my life. Of course, teenage girls are so emotion-driven that logic and reason are practically non-existent. Both my mother and father had cheated on each other. They filed for divorce, and my father moved out. They both were dating other people and seemed to be loving their newfound freedom. That is when the molestations began. My parents appeared to be too busy with their problems to notice what was happening to me. The door was left open, and I was left vulnerable.

Engaged In this dialogue with God in the dark in my car on a side road, I was about to realize my entire life was lust controlled. I still couldn't come to grips with this in my mind. Why would I think God would say such a thing to me? Then just as suddenly as all of this had begun, I realized I got sucker-punched in my stomach. Wow! My life was and had been controlled by lust. Maybe not my lust. But then again? Perhaps that was at the root of many stupid decisions I made. Indeed, other people's desires, as well as my own, had brought me to every horrible circumstance I have ever found myself in. I had made too many wrong choices. So many wrong decisions.

I was on the rebound shortly after my ex-husband filed for divorce after almost 25 years of marriage. So, what did I do? I made a foolish decision. I decided to get involved just one year later. I allowed myself to get involved with a man. I was always a faithful and good wife. Now I was alone, single, and feeling rejected. Then lust raised its ugly head in my life again. I made a very wrong choice in getting involved with this man.

I was in too much pain and confusion to make any decisions. I remember feeling so undesirable. I felt like my femininity was non-existent. I felt fat and ugly. Look at me, I have stretch marks left over from childbirth. No wonder my husband left me, I told myself. I was a Petrie dish of hurt and pain and self-loathing. On top of all of this, I felt foolish. How did I live with my husband, now ex-husband, for 25 years and not really know him? I was still in shock that this had happened. Enter the germ, I mean man, into this Petrie dish. I was ripe to be deceived, and pain and shame were ready for me to experience once again.

At first, I thought it was great that somebody desired me, and he was ten years younger than me to boot. However, that relationship brought me nothing but remorse and shame. Was that lust? Uh, yes! Was it vulnerability, yes? Is there a difference? All of these thoughts and images began to bombard my mind. The realization of pain accompanied my decision to give in to fleshly impulses. The pain is real for both the victims of lust and the one who gives in to their flesh. There was indeed enough guilt, grief, and shame to pass around for everybody. My mind was full of thoughts of the past, the present, and even my future. Where and when was this going to end? What was I doing?

At that moment in time, sitting in my car, I realized all these questions. My mind was racing. What rapidly ran through my mind was that lust has been the essence of humanity's problems since the Garden of Eden. It has always been about the desire of the eyes, whether flesh, greed, or food. Many fallen men and women of God have been victims of the lust of the flesh, whether King David or King Solomon, Samson or televangelists, politicians or teachers, or kings and kingdoms – all destroyed by lust. It didn't matter whether victims or perpetrators. Lust has been the catalyst behind it all. I believe at that moment sitting in the car on the side of the road, talking to God. That He wanted me to write this book. My mind sped quickly to my mother and the conversation at the cemetery with the man who needed counseling. As I remember, so much of the pain of my childhood was a projection of my mother's own grief. When she disdained or rejected me, it was herself that she hated. Why? That is not too difficult to figure out once you know the entire story.

So now, I must tell her story and mine to understand the hope in this book. The dots must be connected not just in my life but in yours as well. What is my mother's story? She was the oldest of six children, and her mother died at the age of 28 when my mother was only 11 years old. That would have would have been tragic enough, and I wish the story had ended there. But tragically, it did not. The unthinkable happened on the day of my mother's own mother's funeral. As my mother lay sobbing on her bed, her father entered her bedroom shortly after that day's emotional trauma. She thought he was there to comfort her. He would comfort her and tell her everything was going to be ok. He sat next to her on her bed and rubbed her curly blonde hair. She was a little beauty with her cotton top blonde hair and green eyes. Her eyes were now puffy and swollen from crying all day. He said he had something to tell her. He began with these words; I am not your father.

She later told me that she was sick to her stomach at that moment. Her mind could not comprehend the words she had just heard. How could this be possible? He was the only father she knew. However, she had never known him to be a kind man. He was abusive to her mother, which is more than likely why her mother died at only 28 years of age from kidney failure during the birth of child number six. Despite the raging fevers and kidney infections, her mother had never received medical attention. Could this not be her father? That made no sense, but why would he lie, she asked herself. She had just lost her mother and now her father too.

She would soon find out that she was another man's daughter, and her mother and stepfather were married when she was only eight months old. Why had she never been told this life-altering truth? But what my mother was about to experience next was far worse. Her biological father had rejected her and never wanted her, even before she was born. I am confident her mother wanted to spare her that pain.

Who could blame her? Then after sharing with her some of these facts, her stepfather raped her.

Dear God, why had I never thought of any of this before? My own mother's birth was even an act of lust. Lust has a way of eating at your soul and causing you guilt and shame that should not belong to you. My mother carried this with her for her entire life. It is crucial, and we must remember we have an adversary or enemy who in his heart says as quoted in Exodus 15:9, NKJV:

> The enemy said,
>
> "I will pursue, I will overtake,
>
> I will divide the spoil;
>
> My desire shall be satisfied on them. I will draw my sword,
>
> My hand shall destroy them."

My mother did have an adversary determined to destroy her life. I am not even mentioning the lives of future generations. As you can see, these situations pass from generation to generation. By definition, this is what is known as a generational curse. A person in one generation is abused or exploited. While not understanding the pain or the answer, they pass the curse on through their behavior, bitterness, rage, or even a false arrogance to generation after generation. How is this even possible? Did you know most behaviors and attitudes are learned and are not hereditary? How is it taught? We will discuss this more later.

So now the door was wide open. I have no way of knowing now when it opened. I don't even know how many previous generations it had fallen upon before it affected me. How was this controlling force of lust spread upon my mother's mother, Pauline, my grandmother? I do know the pain was now about to spread rapidly. I wish my mother had known that our heavenly Father didn't stand by and just let it happen. Her stepfather had made a choice, and we are all given the gift of free will. He chose to walk into her room that fateful night. Perhaps he had been molested as a boy himself. I do not know. I do know most perpetrators have been victims themselves. That does not excuse it, but it is factual. If she only could have realized that the Lord stands at the door and is always with us. He is waiting for us to turn to Him for healing and complete restoration. I know because not only have I seen it thousands of times. I, too, am a recipient of His healing love and restoration of my broken heart.

He stands at the door to heal us and help us, and His heart breaks for us. He sees everything that has ever happened to us.

My mother never went to church or was very spiritual while I was growing up. I believe her anger was turned toward God and not upon who it should have been, her real adversary. I have made the same mistake. I have been so enveloped in my own pain and brokenness that I could not see or understand that God was still with me. Much less close to me. How could this happen if God was close? The Bible says:

> For all that is in the world – the lust of the flesh, the lust of the eyes, and the pride of life – *is not of the Father but is of the world*. And the world is passing away, and the lust of it; but he who does the will of God abides forever.
>
> –I John 2:16-17, NKJV
>
> You number my wanderings; Put my tears into Your bottle; Are they not in Your book?
>
> –Psalm 56:8, NKJV

> Come to Me, all you who labor and are heavy laden, and I will give you rest. Take My yoke upon you and learn from Me, for I am gentle and lowly in heart, and you will find rest for your souls.
>
> –Matthew 11:28-29, NKJV

These scriptures all say that He is there.

Do you know we are never alone, but we feel very isolated when lust is at the helm of our life? Pretend for a moment you and your life are like a ship at sea. Lust is at the helm steering your ship (life). Lust will also act as the rudder, hidden just under the surface. Both on top and bottom steering, unbeknownst to you, towards dangerous rocky waters where you crash into other ships (lives) and sink their ships and yours. That is how unhealed trauma works. Isolated on this ship is where my mother was after the rape. It's as if her life was on a freefall, and there was nothing there to break her fall. She didn't know where or how to get the healing she so desperately needed.

CHAPTER THREE
THE PAIN IS THE DOOR TO OPEN PANDORA'S BOX

A couple of weeks after her stepfather raped her, she went to stay with her aunt for a few days. Her aunt noticed that my mother was highly withdrawn and sullen. Naturally, her assumption was that my mother was grieving over the recent loss of her mother. Her decision to speak with my mother regarding her grief was the opening of Pandora's box. My mother broke down hysterically, weeping after much questioning, and told her aunt the inconceivable had happened just hours after the funeral. Her aunt was horrified and sick. Her uncle wanted to grab the other children and go kill the man. After that horrendous moment, the shock echoed in their minds. Then reason took over, and her uncle called the authorities. Her stepfather was found and then arrested.

The trial was the beginning of a nightmare for everyone involved. My mother had to testify to the judge about what had happened to her. When she testified in the judge's chambers, he asked her if she was pregnant. She was so young, and she didn't understand. Her response to the judge was "Yes, once a month." This response drew a chuckle from some in the chambers. The judge seemed so disgusted; my mom thought he was disgusted with her. She thought she was stupid and had said something wrong or, worse, did something wrong. I am sure he was angry at the circumstances, not at her. After all, she was 11 years old. However, her young mind did not understand. The judge then asked the clerk if she would explain what he meant to this girl. Mom told me she really thought she had done something wrong. Once again, someone else's lust was at the root of my mom's pain, shame, and guilt. But how is an 11-year-old going to figure that out?

What's Lust Got To Do With It? Everything! Unfortunately, the tentacles of lust were about to affect all of my mother's siblings. Her stepfather pled guilty and served ten years in prison.

Then all the children were scattered to various foster homes or orphanages. My mother went to live with her aunt, who had made the gruesome discovery of the rape. However, her aunt and uncle simply could not afford to take on the other children and all those extra mouths to feed. After this man, her stepfather was released, he told the siblings that their older sister had lied and sent him to prison. Can you imagine the pain this lie caused my mother? Her half-sisters and brothers hated her and alienated themselves from her for many years. Do you see the devastating generational impact on so many lives perpetrated by one man's decision to act on his lust?

Fast forward to me at just under 13 years old. My mother's half-brother, 26 years old, needed a place to stay. He called her after years of being separated. My point here is this: do you think my mother could turn down her long-estranged brother? I doubt it. What an opportunity for her to reconcile after so many years. I suspect that she never considered I was in harm's way. That, my friends, is how generational curses are handed down from one generation to another. Neither the victims nor the perpetrators are aware of what might happen next. Are these curses real? I can tell you that they are. We are doomed to repeat history unless we stand up to confront it. In a way, we all are victims, and all suffer in one way or another.

While it is said that hurting people hurt people, I am sure my half-uncle, in many ways, was a victim himself. Growing up in orphanages and foster homes must have been painful. He may have even been a victim of sexual abuse as well. I often wondered if, subconsciously, part of my uncle's plan was to get even with my mother. Remember, most likely in his mind, she was responsible for taking his daddy away to prison. At any rate, he possessed many of the same traits as his father. He was attracted to young girls, just like his father. He possessed a generational spirit of lust, unaware that the pattern was continuing through him. The truth is we rarely recognize the familiar ways that we follow or mimic subconsciously. This is one reason that therapists constantly encourage self-examination.

Studies have shown, as children, 85% of our behaviors are modeled from parents. As adults, far too often, we mimic familiar behaviors that just feel comfortable to us, and we have no idea why? *Unyte Health* clinically defines trauma as this:

> Trauma is the response to a deeply distressing or disturbing event that overwhelms an individual's ability to cope, causes feelings of helplessness, diminishes their sense of self, and the ability to feel the full range of emotions and experiences. [1]

One can only imagine how intensified the trauma becomes when you add to the equation a child's inability to grasp what is happening and who has no sense of control. As children, we tend to believe that authority figures are always correct and that we must be wrong. Heck, we believe as children that some jolly old overweight guy in a red suit comes down a chimney (which he could never fit down) and brings us toys. Or what about that some giant bunny drops off baskets of candy at our houses? Most of us bought it with no questions. Why?

---

[1] https://integratedlistening.com/blog/what-is-trauma/

Because an authority figure told us so. What happens when some adult tells us, as young children, that we are stupid or worthless? I'll tell you. We accept criticism as fact with no evidence. Then it becomes part of our core belief about ourselves. We have no firm grasp of reality as a child; just what an authority figure has told us or projected upon us becomes our reality. The truth of the event and what happened to us is not based upon fact but on what our perception of the event is. That becomes our reality.

If you have experienced this kind of trauma, your first response is that something is wrong with me. You ask, why am I so dumb? Why am I experiencing these kinds of disasters time and again? Why am I making the same mistakes over and over? Why do those I care about hurt me? What is wrong with me? These are natural questions but have nothing to do with reality.

This book will discuss and adjust our core beliefs to a more realistic understanding.

While you may have been a victim of this sort of traumatic event, the good news is you will not live in victimhood. You will be set free from being a victim to being victorious.

As a therapist, I have realized that we all process pain and trauma differently based on our individual experiences and circumstances. Trauma is always based on our perception of the event. Then it becomes the story we have told ourselves regarding the incident. We blame ourselves even though we may be angry at the person who wronged us. Who is to blame is often impossible for us to discern. Our brain is searching for reasons why this happened. We are usually willing to take the blame ourselves. In the therapeutic world, depression is best described as anger turned inward. Anger is defined as unexpressed hurt even when we are the angriest at ourselves, which is the case for most of us. We question ourselves: How did I let that happen again? What is wrong with me? How could I be so stupid? However, our inner shame and anger are manifested outwardly by depression, anxiety, or anger. The problem is how to change this once it has been identified.

Don't worry; I will give you the keys in the following few chapters. Remember, keys only unlock the door when we use them. They are worthless to observe when we have them in our hands and then do not use them. How could I have prevented Pandora's box of pain when it had been opened long before I was even born? Was my grandmother pregnant out of wedlock with my mother? Had my grandfather molested or raped her? Who opened the box? Was it my mother through her pain of being raped by her stepfather, or was it five or six generations ago? Do we ever really know how it started or with whom it started? Does it even matter?

I believe you are already beginning to see the design here in my own family. It may help us to know how it all started to see the pattern, but the most critical information is what we must do to stop it. It has to stop somewhere. It must stop with you and me. If we don't stop the pain and heal, we are doomed to pass it on to our children and grandchildren and who knows how many future generations. We think what happens to us only affects us, but nothing is further from the truth. Even though I didn't intend to, I might add here to this box of pain I passed too much down to my children. My oldest daughter is going to add a chapter to tell her story. It is different from mine and my mother's stories, but nonetheless, you will see the outcome is similar to our lives. Our stories are all different, but the outcome is the same. As you will see in the coming chapters, gone unchecked, lust will take control and run our lives.

CHAPTER FOUR
PAIN HAS POWER, AND SO DOES JOY

The most challenging thing for any of us to understand is *why me?* Why these parents, why this family, why this abuse, why this rejection, why this illness, *why this pain? Why me?* It all seems so unfair! Why is it so easy for some? Why do so many seem to get all the breaks in life? Their lives seem to go so easy and smooth, almost like yogurt in a blender. I always felt like a frog in a blender, trying to claw my way to the top as the blades tried their best to suck me down. That may sound funny, but can you relate? The sun always appears to shine upon some people while many of us seem to be born for trouble, and it follows us everywhere we turn, as relentless as a tornado on our path, purposefully turning our life upside down and determined to bring our house crashing in around us. Have you ever felt like that?

So, it is that most of us refuse to see the value of pain. In fact, we do everything to avoid it. Why wouldn't we? But it can serve us as our best friend if we get the proper perspective! What? Pain a friend? How can that be possible? It hurts, my heart feels broken, my stomach wrenched, and I feel so overwhelmingly lost. How can this pain possibly be a friend or good for me? Pain will either break you or cause you to break through! By changing how we view pain, we will revise the effect pain has on our lives. We have all heard the fitness gurus confess no pain, no gain! Yeah, that sounds great in theory, that is, until you get up the following day after a good gym workout. When we can barely walk and sit, we feel like we just fell out of an airplane at ten thousand feet. That is precisely why most of us believe that if there is no pain. Great, there is no pain!

Greatness is always the fruit of much adversity. Pain will do one of two things in our lives; it will propel us into wholeness and compassion or lead us to the pit of sorrow, bitterness, anger, and resentment. Pain can paralyze us into immobility and stagnation, leading a life unfulfilled and affecting everyone around us and our close relationships. It ignores that by avoiding the pain, we limit our *growth*. Most of us recognize and admire the great overcomers of the world. If we study the lives of great men and women carefully and unemotionally, we find that, invariably, greatness is developed, tested, and revealed through the darker periods of their lives. Author and Speaker, Cavett Robert said, "One of the largest tributaries of the *River of Greatness* is always the *Stream of Adversity*." So, if life has not been fair to you and you have suffered, Congratulations! You are on your way to greatness.

As I realize that *hurting* people *hurt people*! I never recognized that the people who caused me the most significant pain and devastation in my life were desperately hurting people. These people were all hiding behind the veil of arrogance, pride, anger, judgmentalism, and anxiety – basically *pain*.

HUMOR THE HEALER

So much of my life had been shrouded in confusion with deep emotional pain. Yet, I was nicknamed Smiley Wiley (Wiley is my maiden name) in school because everyone said I was always laughing and making others laugh. I was blessed with a good sense of humor. My dad was my mentor regarding comedy. He had a very quick wit.

I liked making people laugh and smile. It made them happy and gave me the desperately needed and desired attention. At a very young age, I learned to mask myself and my insecurities by hiding behind a veil of humor. Humor fulfilled an inner need to be someone accepted. Who doesn't want to be around someone who can make them laugh? To me, it was a win-win situation. However, unbeknownst to me, it was humor that was healing my soul and keeping me whole. It is incredible how healing humor is to the soul. The Bible says, "A merry heart does good like a medicine" (Proverbs 17:22, NKJV).

This Proverb is so true as I would later discover that it alters our brain chemistry when we laugh. It also reduces our stress hormones and increases the feel-good hormone endorphin by up to 29%, which likewise boosts our immune system, causing us to be both healthier and happier. I know God wonderfully made us, and I found a very healing solution to pain through humor and laughter.

I often, as a child, would escape my circumstances by daydreaming funny scenarios and then performing them. It would not only make my dad laugh but make me happy to see his face turn red as he would laugh so hard. I remember one sunny Indiana day; I was outside playing in the dirt and clay. I was probably about 8 years old at the time. The house was in farm country in Greenfield, Indiana. My mom told me to play until lunch was ready. As I looked at the dirt and clay, I began to develop a genius plan. At least, I thought so. I took that dirt and clay and created the most realistic and beautiful feces you ever saw with a bit of water. I was laughing all the way from the field to the back door. When I approached the back door, I put my serious face on. "Mommy," I called loudly; "look what I found." I was holding the dirt shaped feces up very proudly for her to see. Her face turned from curiosity to horror in a millisecond. Her face was enough to make me start busting up in laughter as she screamed, drop it, drop it now! I still laugh when I think about it.

If I analyze my clay trick on my mom as passive-aggressive behavior, I guess it was, in a way, getting even for her rejection of me. I believe in finding the humor in her rejection; I was able to keep the wounds from penetrating too deeply. That was not my thoughts or plan, but it helped me, nonetheless. Amazingly, the pain had become my teacher! I have found as a psychologist that children who have gone through trauma will often use humor as a coping mechanism. It is how many of us have survived, including myself.

When you begin to understand the power of the mind, you know that whatever we focus on grows. For example, if you buy a blue car, even though you haven't noticed any other vehicles that particular color previously, I guarantee you that as soon as you drive it off of the showroom floor, you will see that the color car is everywhere. Why? Because your brain is gathering evidence of just how popular your choice was. Your brain has now refocused on finding blue cars. My point is that if we can fill our minds with joy and happy thoughts, we will find joy and laughter in everything in our lives to a greater degree. If we focus on our sadness, our lives will become much sadder. Growing up was a challenge. I had a mom who seemed impossible to please and a father who thought I did nothing wrong. In some strange way, it seemed to balance things out for me:

> Now no chastening seems to be joyful for the present, but painful; nevertheless, afterward, it yields the peaceable

fruit of righteousness to those who have been trained by it.

–Hebrews 12:11, NKJV

God, in His goodness, had been training me.

I needed to see the humor in my life. Laughter had been my healer and my friend. It is healing in every way, even emotionally. It kept the scarring from going too deep. Our attitudes toward what has happened to us are crucial to peace and happiness. We must not take ourselves too seriously. It is most helpful to laugh at ourselves.

PAIN IS OUR BOOT CAMP FOR SUCCESS

Pain is our boot camp training for greatness and success. We must allow it to teach us.

My painful life experiences propelled me to write this book to help others. Don't wallow in it; learn from it, and it will be a great tutor and a friend. Pain is never experienced without it being for some good use. God never wastes a disaster. He will use those troubling circumstances to shape and mold our characters unless we choose to remain a victim and not allow pain to do its perfect work for us. Our discomfort often reveals God's purpose for our lives.

When men and women join the military, they are basically stripped of their uniqueness and become one unit. Proper understanding and self-confidence follow behind the pain and experience of boot camp. It is actually in the mutual suffering that brotherhood is built.

It is what we believe pain to be that makes all the difference. Let's face it; we can all say poor me and cry and lament all day long about all we have suffered and experienced in life.

Does it change anything? The pain can be intense and affect us on many levels if we allow it to be our enemy. But we have the freedom of choice in all things, even in our experiences.

Why is that? Because we choose how we will view those experiences. I opt for the pain to be my friend; it is my helper to succeed, not my ticket to failure and heartache. However, it is still my choice. When was the last time you had a good belly laugh? I mean, tears rolling down your face, sides hurting, laughter? Why not? The truth is most of us take ourselves too seriously, which is to our detriment.

Have you ever considered why you develop scar tissue if you have a puncture wound, deep cut, or injury? It is because of God's design. Scar tissue, like a skin shield, helps protect that area from further damage. We do the same thing with emotional or spiritual pain. We have scars and battle wounds. If you notice, scar tissue is much harder and thicker than normal skin cells. We become thick-skinned, as it were. We do that with our hearts and emotions, too. We allow our past injuries to harden our hearts and affect our feelings. While this response may protect us for a time by keeping us distant or guarded against others, over time, it will hinder us in our lives and relationships if we don't cut the old scar tissue away. Did you know the Bible even gives us instructions regarding this? The Bible says:

> And the LORD your God will circumcise your heart and the heart of your descendants, to love the LORD your God with all your heart and with all your soul, that you may live.
>
> –Deuteronomy 30:6, NKJV

Notice it says *He* will circumcise or cut away the extra flesh in your heart; that is what circumcision is. Why? In order for you to live and love. Hardened hearts keep us from living to the fullest. You can't circumcise yourself. That is why *He* says *He* will do it!

What is it we must do? Surrender to the process. I am going to outline the process in this book. I am sure you will learn how to surrender to the process through these pages. It is a choice. Choose to live. Allow yourself to laugh at your situation, even to laugh at yourself and how you thought. Learn to laugh again. Again, studies have shown that 20 seconds of a good hard belly laugh is worth three minutes of intense hard rowing on a rowing machine as far as your health is concerned. Row, row, row your boat, or laugh, laugh, laugh your butt off on the way to healing. I am not saying don't exercise, but I am saying laugh. Look at the humorous side of experiences when possible. It has been scientifically studied that children laugh 400 times a day while adults laugh about 15 times a day on a good day. No wonder kids are so happy and at peace. Laughter not only has health benefits for the body, but the effect on our minds and brains and the sense of well-being is phenomenal.

What happened to us? Why did we quit laughing? When did we lose hope and allow the cares of life to overshadow the pure joy of just being alive? What an incredible gift it is just to be alive! Lighten up! Laughter is one of God's keys to healing. God reminds us in Matthew 19:14, NKJV, where His word says: "But Jesus said, 'Let the little children come to Me, and do not forbid them; for of such is the kingdom of heaven.'" What did He mean by that statement, for such is the kingdom of heaven? Forgiving like a child, loving like a child, and trusting like a child is the most powerful way to live and truly taste the abundant life. A joyful life is an abundant life we are meant to enjoy as God's children as part of His kingdom. But it truly is a decision that only you and I can make for ourselves. Proclaim to your heart today – I choose to become childlike in my faith and trust, love, and forgive like a child. I wish to be innocent in my attitude and my heart.

I will never forget the experience I had as a student. While doing some of my post-graduate work, I volunteered some intern hours at a child abuse center. It often seemed the children who had suffered the most considerable abuse were the most anxious to forgive and please their parents. I usually wanted to punch out the parents myself, yet these children were eager to love. But what a fantastic example of unconditional love. Of course, I realize these kids were starved for love and affection, but, wow, I had thought of them often when I needed the courage to forgive and love the unlovable. Jesus said in Matthew 5:44-45, NKJV:

> But I say to you, love your enemies, bless those who curse you, do good to those who hate you, and pray for those who spitefully use you and persecute you, that you may be sons of your Father in heaven; for He makes His sun rise on the evil and on the good, and sends rain on the just and on the unjust.

The truth is children behave naturally the way we should, but we have forgotten how. Now is the time to decide to go back to our innocence, to learn how to live before our brains got rewired by trauma to respond negatively. We will talk in another chapter about how to change that wiring. The absolute truth is we have lost the art of innocence, and in losing that innocence, we have not been able to experience pure joy and liberty in our lives.

The loss of innocence carries a hefty price tag. I know that for a certainty, for I did lose a lot of my childhood far too soon, as maybe you have. I did not lose it willingly, but the price tag was nonetheless colossal. The Bible also says in Proverbs 14:13, NKJV: "In laughter, the heart may sorrow." That was me for many years. Though I laughed, and the laughter did keep the wounds from going deeper into my heart, there was much sadness and insecurities.

I had the wrong perspective regarding my pain. The source of my pain was profound, yet no one knew it but me. I had not yet discovered what the root of rejection and pain was masking. I had learned how to hide it very well. Only God knew what was deep inside that He would yet uncover. In the uncovering, I have learned many truths. One of these truths is our perception.

How do you perceive the events in your life? It is truly all about our perception. You may understand everything that has ever happened to you as a cruel twist of fate, or you may choose to look at your adversity as your key to success and promotion. Before the root of pain was pulled out of me, I viewed myself and my life as a mess and very unfair. After all, I was good; why would God allow such things to happen to me? Sound familiar? At that point in my life, I saw no purpose behind any of it. Don't get me wrong; I in no way believe God was the author of my pain. Oh, it had an author, but it was not my heavenly father. But now I have often told myself, wow you must be pretty special to God if the adversary has been hell-bent, pun intended, in trying to destroy you. But guess what? I win because I have chosen to win. You win because you decide to win.

Pain and adversity will either break you or cause you to break through, and breakthrough you will if you only choose to believe! While adversity is a chapter or perhaps even a small paragraph of your life, remember it is not your whole book. It will only be as big a part as we allow it to be. How large do you want this chapter to be? The pain and adversity you may have experienced in your life are only Hell's attempt to abort you from your Destiny and from the life you have been destined for. It is your life! While you may not have had a choice in some of the battles you have fought and the pain you have experienced, you get to choose your outcome. You have the power of your pain behind you! *Use It now to become the winner GOD has you called to be!* Never allow hell to accomplish its plan in your life. Ask yourself, "How can I use this to help others?" How will my pain be my platform?

When he was a little boy, my son Greg used to love to play with balsa wood airplanes. You know, the kind made of thin, light wood that is pre-stamped and cut to punch out the wings and slide them through the fuselage, and they can glide through the air and soar. There were times he would play with one for hours, and other times, it might be five minutes, and he would come running into the house so upset because it broke in the wrong place and wouldn't fly very high anymore or maybe not at all. Our lives are often like those little airplanes. If broken in the right place, we might soar higher than ever before. Still, too often, when our life crashes, our broken emotions, and hearts will cripple us, even keep us on the ground and hinder us from loving effectively and soaring, even though that is what we are meant to do. We might also avoid settings where further hurt or pain could occur, even affecting our significant relationships, careers, family, and friends. When you look around, you may see many who have endured very tough circumstances but have not been successful. Because they grounded themselves and stayed in pain and have not used the pain to soar instead.

The good news is this. God can take our broken hearts and souls and totally and completely heal those areas. It is a matter of sanctifying the pain and hurt and allowing God to make it part of our healing salve. I will give you all the necessary steps in your healing process, but you still need God to reveal the deep hidden issues you may not even be aware of. You cannot do it on your own. Trust me. I tried for too many years. God must help you to do it. Only He knows how deep the break is in your soul and where to find it, and He will. But you must be willing. I can tell you it may take a level of surrender to the process that you did not know existed. But how in the world do you sanctify pain? By asking God to take it and even thanking Him for every bit of it because it was meant to destroy you, yet it didn't. Remember, it is your perspective! This is a powerful truth! The fact is – pain has developed your character and made you stronger and better. Ask HIM how I can use what has happened to me to help someone else to heal. Put purpose in your pain.

Write down every hurt on a piece of paper, feel all of it, and don't hide it or mask it. Experience it, scream, yell, or cry it out until you are empty, then let it go, wad up the paper (your pain), or burn it, but let it go! Let the person or people who caused this pain to go also. Then, thank God for it and them! Remember what God's word says in the Book of Ephesians: "Giving thanks always for all things to God the Father in the name of our Lord Jesus Christ" (Ephesians 5:20, NKJV). What? All things? Yes, all things. *All* means *all* in any translation!

Remember what God says in the Book of Romans: "And we know that all things work together for good to those who love God, to those who are the called according to His purpose" (Romans 8:28, NKJV). This affirms the truth: when you know and understand God, your Father, He will make sure that everything that happens to you will work for your benefit and good. Wow! That is if you will surrender everything to Him because you *love* Him and trust Him. It takes all the power out of the circumstances meant to harm you. Now pain can only benefit you. What a powerful truth this is. This power truth will allow you to take any situation in life or people in your life that were meant to harm or destroy you and instead empower you to achieve greatness. Remember, it is your perspective! Your Choice! Your decision!

Remember, too, that the person who may have wanted to harm you or by their actions and caused you such agony has actually helped you to become the strong, compassionate person you are. So, all failure you feel is on them and the effect they had on you.

Too often, we get comfortable in our brokenness and pain. After all, it is the perfect shield against future pain and hurt and a great excuse not to succeed because we might just fear success.

We may even hide from people or have such high walls of defense built around our hearts that no one will ever be able to get close. The sad truth of this scenario is that we ultimately become empty and alone when we carefully guard our hearts. We were created for intimacy. Our hearts always long for actual intimacy. Our desire is to be loved and accepted. Anything less keeps us searching endlessly for completion and significance.

There may be another layer to the fear of success. Many of us are too conditioned to believe that the road to success involves risks such as getting one's hopes up, which often threatens to lead to disappointment. How many times have we felt the excitement of believing there may be hope for our situation and our life, only to have the hopes dashed to the ground and broken under our feet, like shards of glass that sting and cut deeply into our dreams and disappoint us once again? Then many of us, especially if we've been subject to verbal abuse, have been told we were losers or not good enough our whole lives in one way or another. We feel that we will never measure up or be acceptable no matter what we do. We may have internalized that feedback and feel that we don't deserve success. Or those of us who were not abused emotionally or sexually, or otherwise traumatized often associate success with uncomfortable things such as competition and envy. Maybe even worse, we fear that we will fail, and every negative thought or word that has been spoken against us is correct. It's easy to see we can sentence ourselves to a prison of our own making. We are forever imprisoned and immobilized. I personally have longed for more but was too fearful of stepping out from behind those bars and becoming the person I was truly meant to be.

What if it were truly possible to move out of our world of reasons, excuses, and past experiences into a world of possibilities, vision, and purpose? I want to tell you it is not only possible, but it is also ours for the taking. We create our world by what we believe about ourselves. The steps you need to follow in this book will be difficult. But consistency will be the key to reprogramming your brain and, ultimately, to your freedom. It has been said: If it doesn't challenge you, it won't change you. We will change our world if we change our thinking and perception of ourselves. But it takes practice. That is the challenge. I was single for eleven years after my second divorce. I was pretty sure I would never trust another man again. So, what was my solution? Get involved with men, I knew that would never work out. They had issues I knew were too complex to deal with for me. Did I do this consciously? No, those relationships caused me pain. I had to get to the next place if I was going to move forward. I had to realize the truth about myself.

CHAPTER FIVE
REALIZING THE TRUTH

The first thing I realized about myself was, oh my gosh, the shock of shocks, I had trust issues.

One of the most aha moments in my life was when I came to the realization that not everything that happened to me was my fault. It was the fault of events that happened to me, and they did not define who I am as a person. This is Step One in the Seven Steps to Healing and Restoration. That sounds like a reasonable conclusion, right? – especially when you have been violated and abused sexually as a young child. It must be an adult's fault, the one who was the perpetrator, not the victim's fault. Doesn't that seem like a logical conclusion? However, this is not the conclusion when you have been the receiver of this type of abuse. Why, may you ask? It is because we, as human beings, are reason-seeking machines. Our brains continually search for causes and meaning in everything that happens to us. We develop an entire story or perhaps even a novel around the situation. Sadly, we will invent the solution when we don't know or have the answer.

Let me give you an example. My mother seemed to have this aversion to females. True, especially for young girls. She usually called them names, even though they were very young. She often referred to them as little hussies. Where would this behavior come from? Self-hatred is the answer. This attitude came from a story she developed in her mind as a child. It was also her trying to make a reason for how or why it happened. In a previous chapter, I told you my mother was molested at eleven years old by her stepfather on the very day of her mother's funeral. During a rape or molestation of a young child, the child will disassociate from what is happening. In disassociation, the child often becomes somewhere else or someone else. I believe my mother became a very naughty little girl in her mind. She laid the blame squarely on herself in her search for a reason or meaning for what was happening. She thought this happened to her because she was a bad girl; she had caused this to happen. Who knows, her molester may have told her she caused it to happen because she was so pretty. Her stepfather probably told my mother not to say anything to anyone about this, which equates to a child's mind that no one must know because I have done something terrible. Now, look at what I have done. I have brought this shame upon myself and my family; she may have reasoned. It is why her mom died because she was naughty and bad.

I was never able to have this conversation with my mom. I was never allowed to know what she thought or how the processes in her mind worked through this experience. She would become outraged if I brought the subject up, so I learned not to approach the subject ever. My mother's culture did not allow her to speak about such matters. Families kept family issues undercover. If we never talked about them, perhaps they never happened. I do know how I felt, though, regarding my molestation. I felt ashamed and was told I was so pretty that my molester couldn't resist me. Of course, that was supposed to be why it happened. It was my fault. In this process, I was also told I could tell no one what transpired. My uncle led me to believe that my father would kill him. When you are a child, you operate primarily on emotions and feelings. Since I felt so guilty and shameful, this must mean something is wrong with me. Then, of course, if my father killed my uncle and Daddy went to prison for the rest of his life, it would all be my fault.

Isn't it astounding for those of us who have experienced such trauma that we have developed these iron-clad stories surrounding the event, and the stories could be a great fiction novel? Then we set about living our lives as if all these made-up stories in our minds are true. And then, we allow them to affect how we view ourselves, others, and the world around us. The innermost workings of our minds then become evidence-gathering machines. We find evidence in all circumstances that this happened because the fact is that I am wrong, and this is, of course, what I should expect, given who I am. Shrouded in the cloak of shame and self-doubt, we begin to make all of our decisions based upon our false evidence gathering. We have built an impenetrable fortress of this is why things happen to me. I am flawed and not worthy. Nobody loves me. I always get rejected because something is wrong with me. If something isn't wrong with me, why did my daddy leave, or why didn't my parents stay together? It must be me.

On and on the merry-go-round we go. Why? Fear is the basis for this thinking, which is only F.E.A.R. – *False Evidence Appearing Real*. Fear fuels our anger and drives us to be defensive and short-tempered. How can fear do that, you may be asking? Fear triggers an adrenalin response that initiates a fight or flight response in our bodies. What are we afraid of exactly? We fear that our most profound insecurities about ourselves may be true. That is in our stories; we are hopelessly flawed and not worthy of love. We don't deserve to be loved. If people know who I truly am, they won't accept me. Do any of these thoughts sound familiar?

My mother thoroughly believed her eleven-year-old self, brought these circumstances upon herself. Much of her bitterness was self-hatred. Then throughout her life, she began projecting her bad girl image upon all little girls. Even me, as her daughter. She could never come to terms with this happening because she believed a false premise that carried with it guilt, shame, and anger. She was bitter and angry for her entire life. She hated her stepfather. This is true. But the bitterness and anger came from a more profound sense of somehow this is my fault, and no one must know. How does one cope with this kind of understanding? By projecting your "badness" onto others and hiding behind a wall of anger and bitterness.

My mother also kept a very dark secret. I did not find out until I was 14 years old. She had been married at fifteen and had a baby girl. I had a sister, Patricia, whom she had lost at 3 years old to her paternal grandparents. Our mother was 17. She said she didn't know how to fight for her. Did this shame and embarrassment add to her tormented soul? I don't know. It was before she married my dad, and she never wanted to talk about it. Was lust involved here as well? She was so young, alone, and afraid, with no mother to direct her or love her. I can imagine how she felt because, in some ways, my life had replicated her life.

That is one of the seven steps to our recovery. We must be able to realize what happens to me in life is precisely that. Something happened to me. I did not cause it. I did not own it, nor does it define who I am as a person. It happened, and the story I built around it is usually a false narrative. I gathered mounds of false evidence to make a reason out of what happened to me as a child. When our brain is functioning correctly, it has a job to do. We have a conclusion such as I am not good enough. I am not smart enough. Our brain then goes into a search mode to find any evidence it can. The evidence can be true or false; it doesn't matter. We search for even the minor things that could be possible. Perhaps a look someone shoots your direction.

I think that was a look of disdain for me. Whether it truly was or not, that is how we developed a story.

Then someone says, "I like your hair better long." We leap to, "They think I am ugly or don't look good." They think that I lack style. They hate the way I look. That adds up to evidence in your brain to make you feel justified in your feeling of insecurity. It is no wonder we feel inadequate. We live in a hostile world with constant negative reinforcement that is constantly piling on in our minds. It happened, and that is all. It was a situation that had no meaning to who I am as a person. We need to place no reason or emotion to it, especially no story of why. There is no need to think it must mean this.

No blame. Most traumatic events in our lives have happened outside of our control or desire. It was not your fault. When we step out of ourselves and our emotions, it is so clear that this was just something that happened, an unfortunate event, nothing more. This is not something we need to carry as personal guilt or shame. It is not ours to carry.

Freedom at last! At least we are on our way. Remember, for us to be free is for us to live free. We will talk about examining the evidence in the next chapter.

CHAPTER SIX
PAIN REFINES YOU;
IT DOES NOT DEFINE YOU

My mother constantly complained about my hair when I was a little girl. Your hair is so straight. Your hair is stringy and on and on. My mother had very curly hair, so I was the constant victim of nasty smelly permanents. She wanted me to have curly hair, too. I grew up believing my hair was awful. I perceived the criticism as something wrong with me. I did not consider it just her preference. Then one day, as an adult, I sat in a stylist's chair. I heard a question from her that was shocking! What did she ask me? "Would you be my hair model for a stylist's hair show?" I almost fainted! What? I asked her why she would want me. Her response shocked me. "Your hair is perfect," she responded. Her answer to my question was it is not too straight nor too curly. I couldn't believe my ears. She went on to say, "I can get it to style anyway I wanted it to."

Wow! The power of false narratives that we all hear as children. Every bad hair day or day I had; flyways went into my bank of false evidence. I must have spent years stacking up the evidence. My bank of false scenarios made me wonder how many other false scenarios I had built in my mind, believing they were true. See how easy it is to fool ourselves into thinking false statements about ourselves. Of course, this is just a tiny example of what we can do to our self-images in our minds.

The deep dissatisfaction within us is never-ending. If we are tall, we want to be short. If we are short, we want to be tall. If we have blue eyes, we would rather have brown. Have you done this? I think we all have. Do you know what I love about four- and five-year-olds? Children at this age usually have great self-images. The girls are all princesses. The boys are superheroes. Fortunately, they have mastered the correct assumption that they were created for greatness and are to do something significant. Where did we lose that idyllic attitude and wonderment that nothing is impossible?

I can tell you where you and I lost it. We began to absorb negative expectations for ourselves. We started to compare ourselves with others and stockpiled mounds of evidence that we were not good enough. This is the chapter where we will weigh through this mound of false evidence and examine what is wrong and not valid anymore. Of course, this will be a process and may take some time. Your success and the amount of time it takes depends on how much false evidence you have gathered. This chapter, however, will give you the tools to begin the journey.

Now back to my collection of false evidence, I would look at other women and define my body image as short and stocky. Never short and petite. I had my first baby at 15 years of age. I had stretch marks because my body was not ready for the kind of stretching it needed to perform in order to carry my baby. Rather than look at my stretch marks as a matter of fact, I chose to look at other women who had no stretch marks as more desirable and perfect than me. Of course, having an alcoholic husband who pointed this out to me and my other imperfections, for instance, I was getting fat, did not help my self-esteem. His being drunk and gone most of the time did not help with the mounting evidence. I would see other teens my age without some of those marks as more beautiful, so evidence was mounting in my mind that added up to why I couldn't be loved because I was ugly. In addition, my mind had already gathered the evidence of why my parents divorced. I wasn't good enough in that relationship either. Why couldn't they love me enough to stay together? My uncle used to tell me they really don't love you. You are nothing more than a convenient babysitter for them. If this were a court of law, I would have been convicted of not being worthy by the age of 15 years. It appeared that I was not wanted or loved enough by anyone. What stories do we make up and believe? What are some of your stories?

After my divorce from my children's father, I was a single mom who did not have a clue how to support three children on my own. By this time, I was 27 years old. My ex-husband told me I would starve to death because he would not pay child support. So damaged was my self-esteem at this point that I did not know what to believe about myself. I worked three jobs to try to keep his prophecy from coming true. Trust me, it was not easy. I did not understand my life at this point, nor did I understand how all of the rejection and shame were actually beginning to refine me. I got stronger and more determined. I loved my children so much. I wanted to be an example for them. I did not want them to be ashamed of me. Heck, I had enough shame I was carrying already, anyway. I reconnected with my parents when I was 18 years old. We were better, and they understood why I ran away, but they had both remarried, and things were very different. I wanted my children and myself to be the family I constantly desired growing up. So, I had a huge goal to work towards to achieve that desire. If only I had understood, then what I know now. I was using adversity to be better. My children were my motivational tool. They probably never knew what was driving me. That's ok; they didn't need to know. I needed to know.

I decided to go into sales at that time, and I worked very hard to get my real estate license. The sales and marketing training I received then began to help me heal my fractured heart.

Really, you might ask. Yes, it is true. My first broker (boss), when I was starting out in real estate, told me to buy a new car. Crazy, right? However, having that goal before me pushed me to keep improving and improving. I knew I could not afford to get lazy. My kids and my car payment depend upon me. Setting goals helps you get out of you and reach for something bigger than yourself. When you reach that goal, you look at yourself differently and say to yourself, hey, maybe I am better than I thought I was. You will be amazed at the effect that has on your self-image. In one of my courses, I learned to take a picture of myself I liked, tape it to my bathroom mirror, and tell myself every day that "You are intelligent, successful, and beautiful, nothing can stop you from succeeding."

Research has shown we talk to ourselves at about 120 words per minute. That can add up to as much as 40,000 to 50,000 words per day! I was learning the art of positive affirmation without even realizing it. That's a whole lot of talking. Think about a Monday morning when you wake up and say to yourself, "Oh shoot, it is Monday. I hate Mondays. I bet it's going to be a chaotic day at work. What am I going to wear? I wish I hadn't eaten so much this weekend. I feel fat." That sets our feelings about the day in a very negative frame. It matters what we say to ourselves. In a previous chapter, we discussed how our brain works to gather evidence to make what we think is a self-fulfilling prophecy.

Let me expound on that somewhat here. Think of your mind and thoughts as the Godfather, the kingpin, the Boss. You tell yourself (your mind) "I can't do this?" "I am not talented enough or smart enough." Your thoughts are the Boss. Now your subconscious is the Mob, the gang. You just told your mind; the Boss then tells the Mob (your sub-conscience) to make this happen. The Mob kicks into high gear, jumps into their limo, and says, "Ok, Boss, we will make this happen." You might as well just go ahead and put some cotton balls in your jowls and play the part well. Marlon Brando would be proud. We must get a hold of and stay aware of our self-talk. Why? Because it is the Boss. The Mob (subconscious) will make happen whatever you tell it. That is how our brain works. Now let's change the Boss to a Boss that says to your mind I believe you are intelligent and capable. Boom, the Mob moves into action to make it happen for you!

You are talented and more than competent; you have got this. We may not always get what we want, but what we get is what we expect. If we can talk to ourselves and lift our expectations, we can improve our outcomes. You may be telling yourselves now that it can't be that simple. Clinical research proves that changing our mindset changes our outcomes. We are indeed masters of our universe. We have the power to create or to destroy.

To begin, let's focus on our minds, on changing the core beliefs that we may have about ourselves. I know this works. How do I know? I have done it. Suppose you had told me as a runaway teenager, a mom at 15 years old, that I would one day be a psychologist and I would write a book. My old self would have told you that you have a screw loose. That would have been an impossibility for the old me. But not the now me. What changed? Did my talent change? Did my ability change? No, I will tell you what changed. My mind changed, and how I think changed. This changed my core belief about myself. I went from believing, "Gosh, life really sucks, and I am stuck with whatever it wants to give to me." Wow, anything is a real possibility if I change how I think about things and myself. Now I have the power to change whatever happens to me for good. Don't get me wrong; I still have days when I think gosh, this really looks futile. But now I know what to do. When life throws me a curve, I know how to use my brain to empower myself. When I have those negative thought patterns, I catch them quicker. It does take practice.

We have what is known as neuro pathways in our brains. They are like many roads or ruts in our brains that take us on the same thoughts or ways we have always done things or behaved. Have you ever been driving home from work, and your mind is a thousand miles away? Suddenly you pull into your driveway and think "How did I get here? Did I stop at all the stop signs?" That is your brain taking over, going to those same neuro pathways that have been created in your brain by constant repetition. Basically, it is the same way we learn how to walk. We do the same thing repeatedly until it clicks, and off we go. We don't have to learn to walk again.

The beautiful part of our brain being like a computer is we can reprogram it through repetition and giving it new information. We don't have to act or think the way we used to. By catching ourselves when we say negative, unproductive things to ourselves, we can change how we think by doing that repeatedly over and over until we develop new neuro- pathways or ruts. By repetition, we will have another autopilot that will take over.

This is why a sports coach will have his players practice the same plays repeatedly until they become very automatic. When the players are on the field, they will automatically perform. Practice does make perfect. It is like learning to ride a bike. The more you ride it, the more it becomes automatic to regain your balance and you don't even have to think about it anymore. We can just ride. You and I must put this method of catching our negative thoughts and the practice of thinking through and talking to ourselves differently.

The more you silence the inner critic, the more the voice of encouragement will be your predominant thoughts. You are literally rewiring your brain through your consistent repetition. I promise you it will work. Truth and understanding changes your life. "Know the truth and the truth will set you free" – and with knowing the truth also then comes knowledge and understanding as well. After that we must act upon that knowledge for truth to work for us.

If you can alter your brain and find your true self once again, isn't it worth the effort? Who were you before trauma? I know I was a different person before my parents' divorce and the trauma of molestation. I was truly at peace and confident, full of joy before trauma invaded my life. That is when joy and peace became elusive to me. Self-doubt and overwhelm was taking over my mind. These are the techniques I used to regain the true me. But in the beginning, I was without these tools. Maybe the pages of this book is the answer you have prayed for.

CHAPTER SEVEN
REALIZING THE POWER OF SELF THROUGH FORGIVENESS

The problem with ourselves is that we need help to stay empowered and focus on essential things and cast aside the things that aren't productive. I have focused that in the dark hole of negativity, and it did nothing but add to the darkness. There is no moving forward in darkness and shame.

There is a powerful verse in scripture that the Apostle Paul tell us in Philippians 4:8-9, NKJV:

> Finally, brethren, whatever things are true, whatever things are noble, whatever things are just, whatever things are pure, whatever things are lovely, whatever things are of good report, if there is any virtue and if there is anything praiseworthy – meditate on these things.
>
> The things which you learned and received and heard and saw in me, these do, and the God of peace will be with you.

This verse concisely gives us exactly what we need to meditate upon. We need meditation to change and heal our minds and hearts from the devastation of pain, rejection, and trauma. The Apostle Paul is telling us here to forget what we used to be or how we thought. Take the time every day to reflect on everything good and praiseworthy, including your progress. Even baby steps that move us forward are still progress; celebrate the small victories. Learn to let go of the negative things you are holding on to.

Focusing on the past hurts and the pain others have caused us creates negative energy that is constantly playing in the background. This negative energy causes us to feel down, discouraged, and sometimes angry. Clients in my practice often ask me, "How do I let it go?" That person who hurt me doesn't deserve my forgiveness and that is true. I didn't forgive my uncle, husband, or even my mother and father because they deserved it. I did it because I deserved it! It is time to forgive and surrender the shame to the one who promised to carry it.

Picture in your mind's eye, if you will, a long rope. In my case, imagine my mother holding on to the rope right behind me. I am holding on to the beginning of the rope. My dad held on to the rope behind her; my uncle, my first husband, held the rope behind him. My second husband and the illicit affair I had after my divorce, he held on behind him. Then every other person who has hurt me. Let's make the rope long enough to include my ex-husband's love interests. Let's get a little longer rope to include friends who have betrayed me. Any guess who is at the end of the rope? It is me. Oh, you thought I was at the beginning of the rope. Yes, I am. I am also bringing up the rear because I have been the most challenging person in this line to forgive. I think we all have experienced that the most difficult person to forgive is ourselves. We ask ourselves so many questions. What am I stupid/ How did I not see this? Why did I allow this to happen? I should have known better. The list goes on and on. It is practically endless. This continuous trying to make sense of something that makes no sense makes it very difficult to let go of the past. Now let us return to me at the front of the rope. When I don't forgive those that hurt me, I am essentially dragging all these unforgiven players into my life, my relationships, and my career. No wonder it is hard to move forward and achieve what I am called and destined to become.

Who is on your rope? Take a deep breath here and be totally honest with yourself. Complete honesty with ourselves is an important step. Compile a list of the people that are on your rope. Identify the one who is the most dominant on the rope. This would be the person who has hurt you the most deeply. Then could you ask yourself how I can release him or her? What if it is to your benefit to let them go? Then one by one, we surrender them. We must let them go. We fool ourselves if we say no; I am making them accountable. No, that, unfortunately, is not how it works. They probably aren't even aware they are bound to this rope that you are dragging behind you. The truth is they likely let go of you a long time ago. You are carrying the burden of unforgiveness. They are not. I hope this paints a clear picture in your mind. Remember that this will be a process that may take some time.

My mother held on to the unforgiveness of her stepfather her entire life. Did it serve her well? No, of course not. It caused her a great deal of pain. This pain, when undealt with, turns into bitterness. Then bitterness became anger, which followed her into all of her relationships. It affected her relationship with me and my siblings. It affected her relationships with her grandchildren. Remember I mentioned in Chapter 1 she was married four times? Yes, it affected every one of those relationships as well. Did her stepfather deserve her forgiveness? If I might, I say here, "No! and Hell No!" Now let's step back and look at the outcome of her refusal to forgive. What was the cost to her? A life of anger and bitterness. My question to you is did she deserve that? No, she did not. Is it worth the cost for whomever, even yourself, still hanging onto your rope? I can only fantasize about what my mom's and my relationship might have been without the people on her rope. That includes her unjustified self-loathing of herself. How much happier would she have been? How much more joyful and free would you be? I can't tell you enough what an important step this is in recovery. Without unforgiveness, every psychologist would be out of business because people would be free to be!

There was a time I would confess that I hated my mother. I couldn't understand why she hated me, or so it seemed. My brother could do no wrong, and I could do no right. I often wondered what was wrong with me. I can remember a time as a little girl. I was probably ten years old. We lived out in the country in Greenfield, Indiana. My brother got a two-wheeler bicycle with training wheels for his sixth birthday. I was almost four years older than my brother and never had a bike. So, I started crying that I wanted a bike, too. My mother responded by saying it's not your birthday. We will get you a bike on your birthday. That answer would have been fine, except my brother was born in August. I was born in December. The problem with that was in December, there was usually snow on the ground. More than likely, this was the reason why I had never received a bike. Both my birthday and Christmas were not precisely the bike riding season. Also, December was the reason I was always given for why I didn't get much for my birthday: it was too close to Christmas.

Now, as an adult, I realize this sounds petty, but it seemed so unfair in my thoughts as a child. My dad saw this disappointment as something he needed to try and fix for me. So off to town, we went. My mom was not happy at all, I recall. I was already starting to feel guilty for wanting a bike.

As fate would have it, my bike would not fit in the trunk because it had to be a 24-inch bike. My brother's bike was only 20 inches, at that time we had a rag-top Pontiac convertible. As might be expected, my dad tore a hole in the convertible top while trying to make it fit in the back seat and still give my brother and me room to ride. Well, again, as you can imagine, the proverbial crap hit the fan. My mom and dad fought all the way home, and my new bike ownership quickly lost its glitz and joy for me. I was not so excited about my prized possession now. My mom was yelling at my dad that Debbie always gets what she wants. She always gets her way. I recall thinking, no, I don't. I would have had a bike long ago if I had always gotten my way. Of course, I knew better than to verbalize those thoughts.

Another one of my early childhood memories was my mom and dad fighting about me. I was probably about four years old. We were living in Kentucky at the time. My parents and grandparents were all born and raised in Kentucky. My father had just returned from a trip to Indiana. I remember being so happy to see him! He had gone there to find a better job and career. I recall running to his arms as fast as I could as he got off the bus. He picked me up and whirled me around. Both of us were laughing. Poor Daddy, I guess in my mother's eyes, that was the wrong thing for him to do. He should have run to her and my little infant brother before picking me up. I remember my feeling of deflation as my mom was yelling at my father. She said the only reason you came back for us is because of her! That was just one of many experiences that built my resentment toward my mom.

I remember often thinking, why does she have to spoil everything? These nagging thoughts are precisely how I felt as we drove home with my new bike. Upon returning home, adding insult to injury, I jumped on the bike and just took off riding. I was filled with such an incredible feeling of accomplishment for a brief moment. I was riding! No training wheels or any assistance is needed! I looked back at my parents to make sure they saw this unprecedented act of skill and smacked straight into a tree. Of course, I did. Then, as I jumped off the bike, dang it, the fender and headlight were dented, and so was my ego because my mom was upset with me and yelling at my dad – I told you it was a waste of money. As a child, I equated that to mean I was not worth the money or the effort. It wasn't that my mother was ever physically abusive to me. She was not. However, incident after incident, as I just described, she helped me build stories in my mind of inadequacy. Not actually building the stories but supplying the brick and mortar. Needless to say, I ended up resenting her tremendously.

When my parents were divorced, I blamed my mom. When my uncle began to molest me, I blamed her. She became my scapegoat for all my pain for many years. Then many years later, as I was in the field of psychology, I realized she was a victim, too. All of her hurt and pain also needed to be directed. I was in some ways her scapegoat. The unfortunate thing about unforgiveness is we can use it as a weapon to hurt the ones we love. The reality is I loved my mother, and I believe she loved me. Being in the midst of unforgiveness hinders our ability to express genuine love. We fear vulnerability, don't we? In many ways, exposure of ourselves means we could be hurt. At the same time, my mother expressed her unforgiveness behind a wall of bitterness, anger, and sarcasm. My mother had no idea how much the events were damaging our relationship. She was too consumed behind her wall of self-doubt and shame. She was a victim of her own story. I also hid behind my primary wall, and still do sometimes, of humor and sarcasm. For me, these are safe. Whenever things get uncomfortable, I make a joke about it. I feel compelled it helps release the tension of the moment for me.

There is more negative power in unforgiveness that I haven't even discussed yet. That is what lust has to do with it. Lust, a negative power, creates walls of unforgiveness and shame that stand between us and those we love. It divides us and pains us. That is the power it holds to attack our physical bodies with chronic illnesses and diseases. We often hear how stress is a killer. When we allow ourselves through some false narrative, we deserve not to have to forgive this person. We have no idea about the tremendous amount of stress that causes us to experience within.

Unforgiveness and bitterness, according to studies, have long been linked to arthritis and cancer. Did I mention that my mother died of ovarian cancer? The unforgiveness and bitterness she held onto her entire life – did it finally begin to turn on her? Is what was eating her starting to eat at her in an authentic, physical way? I am not sure, but I wonder. I remember when she was on hospice, basically her death bed, I asked my mom whether she could just forgive her stepdad. I didn't want her to take that with her to the grave. Her response crushed me. I will never forget her answer. Her shocking response to my question was, I will never forgive that S.O.B.! I didn't spell it out in order to keep this book PG-rated. Did he deserve her forgiveness? As I stated earlier, no. But my mom didn't deserve this burden of shame either. The most outstanding comfort to me is that I know Jesus saw it all and understood her pain far better than I do. Jesus can know precisely how we feel because He is there and understands why we respond the way we do. Why on earth would anyone hesitate to forgive, considering all the benefits? It is because forgiveness is not easy, especially when so many emotions are attached to the offense. Let me share with you what Harvard University studies say.

One of the best ways to practice forgiveness is with the REACH method. REACH stands for Recall, Emphasize, Altruistic Gift, Commit, and Hold. Here is a look at each step:

Recall: The first step is to recall the wrongdoing objectively. Visualize the person and situation and all the feelings that come with it. Don't push aside anything, especially if it makes you feel angry or upset. The goal is not to think of the person negatively or to wallow in self-pity but to come to a clear understanding of the wrong that was done.

Empathize: Next, try to understand the other person's point of view regarding why he or she hurt you but without minimizing or downplaying the wrong that was done. Sometimes the wrongdoing was not personal but due to something the other person was dealing with. "People who attack others are sometimes themselves in a state of fear, worry, and hurt," says Dr. VanderWeele. "They often don't think when they hurt others, and they just lash out."

Altruistic gift: This step is about addressing your own shortcomings. Recall a time when you treated someone harshly and were forgiven. How did it make you feel? Recognizing this helps you realize that forgiveness is a generous gift that you can give to others.

Commit: Commit yourself to forgive. For instance, write about your forgiveness in a journal or a letter you don't send or tell a friend. "This helps with the decisional side of forgiveness," says Dr. VanderWeele.

Hold: Finally, hold on to your forgiveness. This step is challenging because memories of the event will often recur. "Forgiveness is not erasure," says Dr. VanderWeele. "Rather, it's about changing your reaction to those memories."[2]

After forgiving, when the bad feelings arise, remind yourself that you have forgiven, and ultimately, you want good for the offender. If needed, revisit your commitment by reading your journal entries or letters or recalling the shared conversation with a friend. I also add to this and suggest that you pray for the person who wronged you. In our humanity, we often hope that person gets hurt as much as they hurt us. As we are praying blessings upon their lives, we may feel like we don't want them blessed. They don't deserve to be blessed. That may be as difficult as it sounds. The truth is we want revenge. Our focus must be that this is best for us. You will reach the point where you begin to realize how free you feel and want that for everyone. I picture myself like William Wallace in *Braveheart,* screaming Freedom! Whenever I need to forgive. That is how empowering it has now become for me.

Now I want to take a little time here and explain what forgiveness is. First, I need to explain what forgiveness is not. Forgiveness is not reconciliation. It can be, however, not necessarily. In other words, if I forgive you, it does not mean I have you over for dinner. It does mean I am not giving the wrong you committed against me any more time, energy, or space in my head. I am choosing to let all that go. Reconciliation may be impossible for you. The person who wounded you may be dead or may not even be interested in communicating

---

[2] https://www.health.harvard.edu/mind-and-mood/the-power-of-forgiveness#:~:text=Recall.,feelings%20that%20come%20with%20it.

with you. That is ok. Remember, this is more about you. You are using your power, your will to forgive. My head, my choice. My power is in *my ability to choose.*

How I forgave my mother was to remember she had been through far more pain in her childhood than I had been in mine. She was primarily unaware of what she was doing, and there was no personal vendetta or motive behind it. I tried putting myself in her position – the pain, abandonment, and betrayal. She had no idea what to do with all of that. She held onto it, which in turn resulted in her anger and bitterness. I thought about it. Is that the result I want for my life? I looked at how it affected all her relationships, including ours. Was it worth it to hold onto the hurt and the resentment? My answer was a resounding *No*!

I am trying to demonstrate the difference between holding onto or letting go of the hurt.

If you read and lived my life, compared to reading or living my mother's life, I think you would choose me hands down. My life was not apple pie and roses, but the peace and joy I have experienced are far greater than hers. If she were here, she would say that is true.

When I was probably in my forties, I decided to just release her from the guilt of everything that happened to me in my life; I decided to just love her for who she was and not expect her to be who I wanted her to be. That was when I realized she couldn't be the nurturing, loving mother I desired her to be. Not with everything she had been through in her life. I had to be straight with myself. She couldn't be the kind of mother I saw her as being to my brother. My brother and I played very different roles in my mother's life. He was her baby, but she felt she was competing with me for my father's affection. I do not doubt that this feeling was because of the rape she endured with her father. I realized the story she was living out in her mind would not change because she didn't know how to change it.

At that point in this process, I realized the choice was mine to make, not hers. I had the power to forgive and let go of my expectations for Mom to be able to make me happy. I let go and tried to show her as much love as possible.

My choice was to seize my strength and dump the unforgiveness I hated seeing in my mom, the unforgiveness that had turned into a root of bitterness. I alone had the power to do that. Is that what I wanted for my life? Of course not! That is not what you want for yourself either! We can't make others do what we need them to do. We only have the power to decide what we do ourselves in our lives.

Forgiveness is our choice to make; it is not about rectifying our past. It is about moving toward our future in true freedom and liberty. Forgiveness is not for the person who hurt you. It is for you.

CHAPTER EIGHT
WHEN I DON'T RECOGNIZE MYSELF

My second divorce was from a man I had given the most part of my adult life to. I'll call him Edward for the sake of anonymity. After my divorce from him, I felt so lost in many ways. I had built a life with him for 25 years; I no longer knew who I was. I had spent the last twenty-five years being a part of his life and always thinking about what he wanted; I had thought, at long last, this was going to last forever. During our marriage, I had lost myself along the way. What did I like to do? Did I want to be in ministry anymore? Did I want to be a therapist anymore? Did I even have a vision, or was my vision really Edward's vision? What did I even enjoy doing for recreation? I felt as if I had been like a genie in a bottle, and his wish was my command. I had always wanted to make him happy. I rarely considered what I wanted to do. Although I knew I was called to help people, betrayal had even made me question that.

We had been living in what I believed was our dream house for ten years. We had a beautiful home on a hill with a lake view. I was so sure; this was where I would live for the rest of my life. I loved this home. It was everything I had dreamed of a gated property with a circular drive. A lovely tall fountain in the center of the circular drive. I designed the swimming pool with a waterfall over rocks flowing into the pool with a rockslide for the grandkids to enjoy climbing to the top and sliding into the pool. The pool and jacuzzi were stationed on a beautiful hill behind the house with a perfect view of the lake. When night fell, we could see all the city lights below with the moon and stars reflecting on the lake. It was where often I would go to pray and gain some peace and sense the blessings of God in my life.

But a couple of years after our divorce, the reality was setting in. This house was too much for me to keep. It was my dream, just as having my beautiful family and ministry were all part of my dream come true. Or was it? I had spent much of the last few years of our marriage leading two lives – one life in front of people, another one at home. Not all of the time was it chaos. But far too often, it was arguing over so many things from work. He often would pull back from the counseling center and church responsibilities. He often would say to me, you handle it. Then when I did, he would yell at me. What are you trying to do? Take over? I never seemed to be able to please him. It didn't matter what I did. I could always feel the sharp edges of eggshells under my feet. I remember sitting out by the pool many nights looking up at the stars, realizing I was losing my husband, ministry, and my entire way of life. This was the life I worked so hard my entire life to help build. I felt like a loser and failure. Had I wasted the last twenty-five years of my life? I was about to lose it all, not because I was a bad wife, mother, businesswoman, or pastor. But why? Dear God, why?

What's Lust Got To Do With It? Was there lust going on here? Something I did not yet know or understand? Something was deeply troubling my spirit; I knew that. I forgot how to live and be at total peace. I was so accustomed to living my life covering up for him and his terrible temper. He often slammed cabinets at work in front of the staff if he disapproved of something I said or did. Not always just in response to me, either. Often some of our team dealt with his anger and did not know how to respond. They and I would nervously look at each other with red faces. There were many embarrassing days that he would leave the office angry and burn rubber squealing as he sped out of the parking lot, leaving us in the front office with mouths gaping open, asking ourselves why? I would feel so humiliated that I would walk back to my office, close the door, and cry, thankful no clients were standing in the reception area to witness this behavior.

Then there were other times he would be the office clown, making everyone laugh at his antics. We just never knew. He had two fingers missing on one hand due to an accident. He sometimes drew goofy faces on his nubs and did hilarious puppet shows with them. It would catch everyone off guard, and we would all be cracking up. Sometimes he would stick them in his nose and look like his fingers were to his brain! So, I am not saying that all our times were terrible. They, indeed, were not. We had a lot of laughs because we both were witty and cracked each other up. I am sure many of you can relate. It was no different at home. I never knew which husband I would encounter – the charming and kind man with a great sense of humor or an angry, threatening, screaming maniac. I felt as if I always walked on eggshells. Eventually, this reached the point that the good wasn't outweighing the bad. That is what makes toxic relationships so confusing, and it becomes easy to lose oneself. Here I was a professional therapist who knew how to confront unacceptable behavior. But I found myself in survival mode. I just desired to be as peaceful as possible for as long as possible. So, I learned it was easier and safer to suck it up and endure.

Is there any wonder I lost the honest Deborah somewhere along the way? I always wore the "everything is just fantastic" mask. It wasn't fantastic. My job was to make sure everyone thought all was well. After all, I was the dutiful wife, and he was the senior pastor of our church. His behavior might stumble somebody. How would it look if I let anyone find out? We would be ruined if our community knew everything that was going on.

On the outside, we looked like the perfect family. Our grown children were deeply involved in the ministry. My youngest daughter and her husband were the youth pastors; how does it get better than that? Our grandchildren were all so beautiful and sweet. Who was I to burst everyone's bubble? So, I sucked it up so much that I soon began to believe the lie.

Everyone has problems, right? Whoever said marriage was easy? I was used to not having an easy way to go. I expected more because we both wanted to serve in ministry and lay down our lives for others. That sufficed for a while. Then he would relapse by taking prescription drugs and sometimes getting drunk and going on a binge. Of course, I couldn't let anyone know. We were well-known in the community and were the leaders of a flourishing congregation. I had no one to confide in and tell our deep dark secrets. I didn't want my children to know, as they had come to accept him as their dad. Heaven knows their biological dad was always missing in action. He had never been there for them. I couldn't bear to tell them their mom and stepdad would disappoint them again. I asked myself, what is wrong with you? Here you go again, a two-time loser.

I felt trapped in a web of self-destruction. I couldn't go to our professional friends for help, as Edward and I were far too well-known in our community. If this got out, it would ruin us!

Then, of course, who could I approach in our church for advice without it becoming a scandal? As a result, I became a codependent cover for wrong behavior, and I was never sure what choice I had. I should have known this situation was volatile and about to implode like a skyscraper marked for destruction. The more I tried to cover for Edward, hoping to hold things together, the more my husband spiraled out of control. I am sure you can see where this is all going. I had no idea my husband was also addicted to pornography which took its toll on our intimacy. I internalized this to mean that I must not be desirable to him or anyone. Pornography feels the same to the other spouse as adultery. I know because I have experienced both.

What's Lust Got To Do With It? I was about to find out. Then came the day he told me he didn't want to be married anymore, nor did he want to be in ministry. After that crazy announcement and he left me, I discovered his porn addiction. I also found out that he had been on dating apps for singles. He was corresponding with a couple of the women. I had no idea until the office administrator had to go on his computer to retrieve something. She found out what he had been hiding from me. This information only reinforced my conclusion that there was something wrong with me. I felt so unwanted and ugly at this point. I felt even more betrayed this time.

    You see, the year before this happened and he decided to leave, I had forgiven Edward for having an affair with a woman in our congregation. She was my youngest daughter's age. I cried for weeks. I couldn't understand how he could do this. This infidelity with a younger woman destroyed my self-image as a woman. The way I found out; you may be wondering? I remember that day with total clarity. There was a couple in our office telling us they needed to leave the congregation. They had been with our ministry for several years but were unclear about why. The same thing had just happened a few days before with another couple who had been with us for many years. I felt like there was more to the story than they told us. For the first couple, I felt like this woman was a close friend to me. The subject of trust came up, so I asked her if she trusted me. Her response was "Yes, I trust you," and then I noticed her voice trailed off. I was confused and hurt. Little did I know that these two couples knew a horrible secret that I did not yet know.

I was about to find out in a very shocking way.

    Later that day, I decided to call my youngest daughter, who was also a youth pastor and a worship leader on staff. When she picked up the phone, it sounded like she was crying. I thought she must have heard the news about this latest couple leaving. I remember telling her I didn't understand what was going on. It made no sense to me. I remember she said, Mom, I know what's going on. I don't want to tell you this, but I just discovered that Dad is having an affair with Sheila (I will use this name for her in this book). I remember how my heart froze in my chest with what felt like a knife inside it. I was unsure whether to cry or scream or run into the street! I composed myself and asked her how do you know this? I was honestly hoping, against my better judgment, it was just an ugly rumor. But in my heart, I knew it was true. It all made sense. My daughter had seen an old friend who was Sheila's good friend. Sheila's friend apologized to my daughter and said I am sorry to hear about what happened to your mom. My daughter asked her, "What are you talking about?" The friend apologized again and said I am so sorry to tell you. I thought you all knew what was going on. Sheila told me that she and your dad have been seeing each other for a while. My daughter was sobbing at this point. What a web lust is. How many innocents get caught in the web of lust, betrayal, and pain?

My heart was totally shattered and pained. It physically hurt. I wanted to leave Edward immediately. So many emotions I was experiencing all at the same time – hurt, betrayal, anger.

I was 57 years old. We had been married for almost 25 years. But I kept remembering that I had told myself I would never go through another divorce. How could I start all over again? What about our grandchildren? Our congregation? So many thoughts were swirling in my head. Plus, despite it all, I loved him. When I confronted him with what I knew, he claimed he loved me and would do whatever it took to make it up to me. Then he swore to me it would never happen again. If I had only known, it was going to end badly anyway. I felt I owed myself and everyone to stay and make it work. One year later, I started to trust him again and believed he meant what he had promised me the year before. Then the announcement I don't want to be married anymore. And here we go again? I was done at this point. I knew I couldn't do this again.

When you are living through this, it is not so evident that they have the problem because you are in survival mode. My brain was constantly racing, trying to find some reason that would make sense for why this had happened to me again. I tried to reason in my mind why I should stay. You see when my parents became divorced, I was devastated. I stood looking out my bedroom window at the sky, asking God why. I promised myself that I would never get a divorce when I had children because I knew how much it hurt. But here I was all over again. I had children, grandchildren, and even an entire congregation that would be devastated this time. I felt completely helpless because there was absolutely nothing, nothing I could do to stop it. Here I was once again, asking God why?

Did I mention that in the previous year, before he left, he had become high on prescription drugs one night and had been drinking? This was just a few weeks before my daughter discovered what was happening with Sheila. Of course, He had Sheila on the side before I knew anything about it. We argued because I told him this was wrong for him to be drunk and using painkillers; he should not be doing this. He was a pastor, after all. My speaking up just made him angry. This time I felt brave enough to speak up. Without any wavering in my voice, I stood up to him. Before I knew it, he pulled out his Colt-45 and pointed it at my forehead. When you are looking down at the barrel of a 45, it looks like a cannon. I heard myself saying, go ahead and shoot. I know if you do, I will be standing in heaven in the next moment in the presence of my Lord Jesus. Where will you be?

I believe the Holy Spirit protected me that night. Little did I know he wanted someone else. God is good. He gave me the courage to say what I needed to say at that moment. I would never recommend anyone else to try this. That could have easily been the last day of my life. I had no idea he probably wanted to get rid of me. Don't try this at home.

But now, one year later, from the time he held the gun to my head, and I had forgiven him? Here I stood again. I didn't have a gun to my head this time, but I felt like I was losing my life, nonetheless. My hopes, my dreams, my ministry, our dream home, everything. I knew I had my children and my grandchildren, and my Jesus. I had the most important things in life. But I felt like asking once again   Why God?

How did this happen to me again? Is there something wrong with me? Am I just incredibly stupid? I was asking these questions of myself, what is wrong with me, when I truly should have been asking the question, what is wrong with him.

But those of us who have experienced trauma in our lives are more than willing to take on the shame and guilt ourselves. Can you relate? I want to let you know you are not alone, and the actions of others have nothing to do with you. We can only be responsible for our own actions – no one else's.

CHAPTER NINE
HOW IT KEEPS HAPPENING

I mentioned earlier that my first marriage had ended in divorce, too. In the first marriage, I instigated the divorce. I felt terrible because I knew how horrible divorce is for children. You might be asking why I would file for divorce since I had promised myself that I would never do such a thing. But I had also lost myself in this marriage. More times than I would like to remember, I would load my three kids in the car and search the bars that he would frequent because it was Friday night, and he had been paid. I was desperate to catch him before he spent all his paychecks on drinking and buying rounds of drinks for everyone in the bar. If I didn't find him soon, I would have no grocery money to feed the kids. When I would see his truck parked at a bar, I would have to swallow my pride and be the embarrassed wife that had to walk up to the bar and tap him on the shoulder to ask him if I could have some money for groceries. He would look at me as if disgusted with me for asking. It was very humiliating. The fear and embarrassment at times were overwhelming. I could feel my face flush as all eyes in the bar were focused on me as I left the bar. Sometimes I would hear the laughter as the door closed behind me. When I was safely back to the car, I felt a sense of relief. At least we would eat this week.

Wayne had a habit of disappearing often for days at a time. There were numerous occasions when he would come home with hickeys on his neck. I knew he had been with other women, but I felt trapped in this vicious cycle with three kids and no education other than a GED for high school. But we had been together since I was 14 years old, and I did not know if there was any way out. I had no one to blame but myself. At least, this is what I would tell myself.

One weekend, he did not come home all-night Friday. That Saturday morning, I decided to take the kids swimming at a nearby lake. When I pulled into the driveway, I saw his truck parked in the drive. I felt my heart beating quickly, pounding within my chest. I looked at my oldest daughter, only to notice the fear on her face as she bit her lower lip. I told her to stay in the car with her little brother and sister. I went inside cautiously, not knowing what to expect waiting for me. I was unsure what mood he would be in, and I didn't want to expose the kids to another bad experience. As I walked into the den, I saw him lying on the floor on his side, his face in a pool of vomit.

I can't express the disgust and even hatred I felt inside of me at that moment. I wanted to kick him and scream at him at the same time. I remember the sting of tears flowing down my cheek as I thought, you are so selfish and cruel to do this to the kids and me; I wish you were dead. And then I heard myself saying it out loud. I rolled him over on his back. I heard the kids getting out of the car, and I hurriedly ran out to the car and told them to get back in. I told them we will go and get some ice cream. I will never forget the worried look on my oldest daughter Vickie's face. She knew something was up. I had rolled him on his back, hoping he would choke to death. I know that is terrible. I can't even believe it myself, but I did it.

As we were driving to the drugstore, my moment of truth hit me. My God, what am I doing? I realized at that very moment that this marriage had to end. I was becoming someone I didn't recognize. I would never hurt a fly. But I had just done something that could kill my children's father. This relationship was destroying the real me. I told the kids I forgot something, went back into the house, and rolled him back on his side. We left again to get the ice cream. But everything changed that day. I knew I had to make a decision. I was the kind of person who would not want to ever hurt anyone, and there I was with murder in my heart, just wanting so much for the pain to stop. I would rather see my husband dead than have to endure this again.

I had to admit there were many nights I would lie awake when Wayne hadn't come home again. I thought and even hoped he was in an accident so I would not have to deal with him coming home drunk and having blown through his paycheck again. I finally admitted to myself that I was changing. I was turning into a woman that I did not want to be. There was no way I could continue like this. It wasn't suitable for the children either. I had to make a decision or lose myself. That day, I decided I must get a divorce.

I even hated the word *divorce*. But I had to admit I could see no other solution. I had begged and pleaded so many times for him to quit drinking for the kid's sake. Sometimes he would respond by yelling at me. There were other times he would swear he would stop rather than lose us. There were times he would quit for a few weeks. These times were usually short-lived. I remember one time he quit drinking for an entire year. I remember hoping against hope he had realized this was the way he should want to live, that is to live to be sober for me and the kids. But it didn't last.

I had heard the promises ever since I was 14 years old. I couldn't believe them anymore. However, this was the first time I realized their effect on my character, which made me think about how it must affect the kids. By this time, I was 27 years old. If I had been a little wiser and older, I might have realized the relationship doomed itself from the beginning. I did not understand alcoholism and how it worked. I believe there were times Wayne wanted to change, but he had no tools to help him. His father was an alcoholic also and had abandoned him at a very early age. He was raised in foster homes and had such a horrible childhood that I always felt sorry for him, despite how he treated me. Looking back on it, I realize he probably used the poor-me card on me often, and I fell for it. I was just so desperate not to get a divorce as my mother and father had. I still hate divorce, and I don't believe there are ever winners in a divorce. I have never experienced anything that continued and damaged future generations as much as divorce, sexual abuse, and addiction. However, staying in these situations can lead to possible violence and someone dying. All too often, divorce is the lesser of two evils. So, why does it keep happening? I was very troubled by my life. I felt like a double loser. What was wrong with me? I even used to joke that my picker was broken! But was my picker broken, or was it something else? Was it me? All I knew was I did not want to chance it happening again. I had not studied any neuroscience at this time. I was left with the idea of, "Girl, you are really screwed up."

What does neuroscience have to do with making wrong choices in men or spouses? Psychologists are always learning more about how trauma affects the brain and our decision-making process. Did you know that divorce is one of the most traumatic experiences you may experience? It is right under the death of a spouse or child. If I add the trauma of molestation, the trauma is then compounded a thousand times. So, how does trauma affect your brain? Basically, without becoming too clinical, trauma affects the area of the brain that deals with perception. Our filters get clogged, so to speak. That is when we operate on sheer emotions or feelings. Sometimes we will hook up repeatedly with abusive or toxic people even though we despise the behavior. That is because we feel familiar with and know how to deal with that behavior subconsciously. We sense that familiar feeling of yes, I know how to navigate here. There is also the aspect of making this relationship go right this time.

What to do to stop this cycle? Go through the process and heal before you think about another relationship. This will take work to accomplish. You may need outside help from a therapist or life coach. Following through with the 7 steps in the last chapter of this book will put you on the road to recovery. But never be afraid to ask for help. A friend to work with as an accountability partner is also very helpful. It took me a long time to work through my trust issues, but I can tell you there is trust after trauma and faith after fear! I was healed from all the trauma in my life, and you can be too! I found a wonderful loving husband who just loved me for myself and nurtured our relationship despite me and my insecurities. I never have to walk on eggshells now, and I am free from the shackles of my past. Even though I am not proud of my past, I want to tell you, my story. In retrospect, the sense I can make out of it now is that God will use it to help you and many others.

Part of the solution is Never to Give Up! You may fall seven times but get up again. Do it again.

You may not feel like doing it again, but others are depending upon you. Lust is transgenerational. In other words, it is like a curse that will pass from one generation to the next. Future generations are depending on you. I never thought when I was a fifteen-year-old girl about future generations. But in the next chapter, you will see a real-life demonstration of how true it is!

My daughter Vickie wrote chapter 10 to tell her story of the next generation. Vickie Zenker is a Business and Life Coach; she has coached since 2008 and is currently working in the Real Estate Industry as part of a Leadership team.

She is a conference speaker and writer. Vickie has dealt with many trials in her life and overcame them with the power of God. Her trials have led her to a passion and vision of helping others become over-comers in all areas of life through a focus on God, Grace, Gratitude and Grit. As part of her passion, she has coached for over 13,000 hours.

Vickie says she is honored and humbled every day to share God's word, mercy, and grace as HE has freely given to her. Her prayer is that this book will help others to overcome any adversity and lean into the mercy and grace of God.

CHAPTER TEN
GENERATIONAL CURSES

THE SEQUEL

My mother, Dr. Deb said, "That night . . . at the Miami bridge . . . ready to jump into the cold, murky dark waters below and end my life and the life of an unborn child. God, thank you for your voice on that fateful night, gently yet firmly saying step down and back off the bridge. Do not do this; I have more for you than this. The life inside of you is mine, and it is not yours to take."

That unborn child is me! The oldest daughter. Mom, thank you for listening to the voice of God even when you felt like you had nowhere to turn except to avoid the pain you felt. Who would ever think about the impact of that decision to step away from the bridge and how the lives of future generations would be impacted? When I reflect on the decision my mother faced at such a young age, I am so thankful she listened to the still voice of God. Having teenage daughters, myself, I cannot imagine that moment of standing at the bridge and thinking of taking my life. In fact, my life would be a turn of events that would entangle the web of lust. Who would have thought? Yet I am grateful as my life today is one that I am blessed with. Every day, I have been given the gift of life. Yes, God is there through it all! Mom, God loves you and us more than we can fathom.

All girls and ladies in the world are beautiful daughters of the *KING*. We are His masterpiece. The Book of Ephesians tells us: "For we are His workmanship, created in Christ Jesus for good works, which God prepared beforehand that we should walk in them"

(Ephesians 2:10, NKJV). Despite our decisions, situations, and circumstances, He chooses unconditional love. The Bible shows us that God's unconditional love never fails and is not motivated by personal gain. Also, Romans 5:8, NKJV, says: "But God demonstrates his own love for us in this: While we were still sinners, Christ died for us." I hang onto these thoughts of confirmation. You can see in my childhood experiences and my mom's experiences that sometimes the only hope we can cling on to bring us through is His unconditional love despite our situations and choices. Have you ever had a situation in life that hurt so deeply that you shove it into the recesses of your heart? As my story goes, so does that hurt as a child. Sometimes you do not even know how to deal with the situation you have found yourself in the middle of.

It was an exciting day for me; I was going to get to be with my grandma and then have a play day with a family member. My mom and grandma went out to run some errands. I was four years old, an innocent child. Just a little girl with hopes and dreams; the world was mine. I was inquisitive, happy, and wanted to be friends with everyone. As I was playing, laughing, and bouncing around with a head full of blonde curls and blue eyes, my relative lightly grabbed my arm and said it was nap time. My relative said he wanted to play with me as I lay down. He began to fondle me. He told me nobody likes me, and everyone hates me except him. I did not know or even understand what was going on. I knew no one was supposed to touch my private parts (the part I called my woohoo). I was confused. This family member was about thirteen years older than I was. He stopped, and soon, my mom and grandma were back at the house. I remember telling my mom a member of the family touched my woohoo. I really do not know what happened after that. This incident began the cycle of looking for acceptance, not wanting to disappoint others, and looking for love. As I now recognize, I don't know how as a four-year-old little girl, I could feel as though I disappointed my mom and others. I did feel that way. Maybe it was the look in my mom's eye when I told her, or maybe it was the words, "Nobody likes you"? I can only think it is the cycle of lust and the web of the adversary that it creates. To be completely honest, in retrospect, I began to get really good at shoving hurt and disappointment into the crevasses of my heart. Creating one of my biggest fears, the fear of disappointing others the way I believe I was disappointed as a little four-year-old girl.

This cycle continued throughout my life so much that I looked for the disappointment others caused me. Almost as if I expected it. My father was an alcoholic. I remember most of my childhood years from four to thirteen, searching for him so that we had money for food on the table. Every Friday, I would get a pit in my stomach. I always knew as a small child that weekends usually meant looking for my dad before he spent all his money at bars. There is a purpose for sharing this, as I will explain further.

As part of this normal Friday weekly routine, I remember one weekend in particular. When I was around eleven years old, I begged my dad to come home so that I could have a friend stay the night. Friends staying the night at my house were pretty much nonexistent when I was a child. My dad promised he would come home. My friend came over after school. I was so excited! Four o'clock, 5 o'clock, 6 o'clock, 7 o'clock, and I imagine you can figure out the rest of that story. My mom came to me: "Honey, we need to take your friend home. Dad is not home, and we need to go out." So, disappointment welled up. I knew why, and without any fuss to my mom, I watched as she called my friend's parents, apologized, and just said something came up and we needed to leave for somewhere. My friend was dropped off, and the search began. One bar after another, we drove around looking for his vehicle so we could catch him in time to get money for the next day or days he would not come home. She could not leave us home, as we were not old enough to be alone, and I was not old enough to watch my siblings. So, the trek was one we all experienced, the trek for my dad and money so my mom could feed us, her three kids. How could he lie? He said he would be home so my friend could stay the night. He promised. What do promises even mean anyway?

Something happened to me that night. I began a cycle of bitterness and hurt. I started begging my mom to leave my dad in the midst of all the pain, I still always wanted to be a daddy's girl. Yet my mom was my rock. She was always so calm, young herself, basically raising three children on her own. My mom was somehow able to find the best of every situation and share her unconditional love to her children with joy and humor. She was not afraid of a good shaving cream and whipped cream fight, wet paper towels are thrown at each other, and running through the house laughing. It was that laughter and love that kept us strong. These playful moments often happened in our home. I remember one time, we made a complete mess, whipped cream, shaving cream, and then came the thought – where is the chocolate sauce? Throwing paper towels saturated with shaving cream. Those stick quite nicely to the wall, I might add. When suddenly, we hear a knock at the door. My mom, drenched in shaving cream, whipped cream, and paper towels on her head and clothes, proceeds to the door. To our surprise, I hear a voice saying, "Who is in charge here?" I hear my mom holding back laughter as she responds, "I am, sir." Well, I don't know what that cop thought that night, and obviously, our neighbors thought someone was hurt with all the screaming, yet it is a memory I will never forget.

A reminder: have fun, and don't sweat the small stuff (or even the large stuff). Look for the joy. It is there. God has designed us to be joyous. The Joy is our strength! "Rejoice always, pray continually, give thanks in all circumstances; for this is God's will for you in Jesus Christ" (I Thessalonians 5:16-18, NKJV). Now I can look at these scriptures and know it is sound advice to live by, and it is true. I really do not remember at that age having a true relationship with the Father, our King. So, when my earthly father disappointed me, my mom was whom I knew I could always turn to and count on. For that, I was very thankful.

I was almost thirteen years old when I came home from school one day, and my mom was all packed up and ready to run off with her three children. I remember thinking I was glad and yet so sad and scared all at the same time. Even a little fearful of the unknown yet relieved of the weekly disappointments I had come to expect. My brother was four years younger than I was, and my sister was almost four years younger than my brother. They did not really understand. They often did not see or experience the same disappointment I did – or so I thought. That day we left, I pushed and placed yet another wall around my heart. See the patterns? *What's Lust Got To Do With It?* Everything. It began who knows how many generations ago. There is hope; we can be encouraged. No matter what we go through, *He* is with us through it all. God never says we will not experience pain, loss or hurt; He says *He* is with us in the midst of the fire. Let me tell you, as I have lived out situations in my life, it is *TRUE*!

Here I am, a teenager, thirteen years old, and having experienced molestation at a young age, loss of what I dreamed of as a family, then hormones, emotions, and disappointment kick into high gear. Still not in a relationship with God. All I knew was that there was a God, and yet I did not feel Him or know Him. My mom and dad divorced, and still, my heart as a child desired the relationship of a father and daughter, even though it usually would involve hurt. My granddaddy helped my mom buy a house, and she worked three jobs so that she could provide for us and buy us clothes. I remember my mom always wanted the best for us, and she would do all she could to give us our heart's desire. Not all the time, yet she wanted to be able and give us some of our wants as she always provided our needs.

As she was working her third job one day, my dad called and talked to me. He seemed as if he had changed; he seemed as if he loved us all. He just wanted to talk to my mom one day. I thought it would be ok. It was just a conversation. All should be good, right? I called my mom and told her how Dad loves us and just wants to talk to you. I remember asking Mom if she would please talk to Dad. I said he wants to meet you when you get home and just have a conversation. Mom, he wants to apologize, I said. She said she would meet him at the house when she got home. He came over and spent time with us shortly before she returned home. When she got home, everything seemed normal; he told her he wanted to speak with her in the bedroom. After a few minutes, the next thing I know is I hear noise in the back room, a huge smack, and a struggle. I ran through the hall with my heart sunk and saw my dad hurting my mom. Back in the day, when we had actual telephones with cords attached to the wall, I ran to the telephone, picked it up, and yelled, I am calling 911. Leave my mom alone, and I am calling the police. He ran out of the back room to me and wrapped the cord around my neck. As I screamed and kicked, he let go. He then picked up my sister and threatened to take her. As I screamed the words that they were on the line, he eventually, as I remember, threw her to the ground and left.

Sheer terror hit my world, and I was screaming and crying. What have I done; I am such a disappointment. I told my mom it was ok. What have I done to my mom, my rock? I allowed her, my sister, and my brother all to get hurt. The very thing I feared. After being disappointed, I then turned around and disappointed others. How could this happen, I thought? How could I be so wrong? How could my dad do this? Even worse, how could I let this happen? Once again, hurt and disappointment shoved down into the crevasses of my heart. Another wall is being built. Shame and guilt for hurting my family. Maybe if I had not begged my mom to leave my dad, this would not have happened, or maybe if I had not talked to my dad, this would not have happened, or yes, maybe if I were not selfish to have a daddy, this would not have happened. It happened, and the plan was not to place shame and blame on me. Yet in my world, that is the story I told. Give me another reason to look for disappointment in future situations. Something I have learned is when you look for evidence, you will find it, or it will find you. I am not saying I deserved or even caused any of this as a child; however, the situation and experiences gave me a reason to look for disappointment. After all, I have been dealt that so far in my thirteen years of life. Or was it the situations and experiences of future generations that made their way into my life? Either way, we can be the victor.

As I continue to go through my life, I know that the fateful night on the bridge where my life was spared is a complete blessing. The lessons in my life have helped so many, and it is my prayer that this small piece of the story will continue to help others. Fast forward a few years, I continued to love my dad at a distance, gathering from every situation, looking for disappointment, and shoving them into the recesses of my heart, basically building fences along the way to build a "Fort Knox" around my heart. Allowing the root of bitterness to take hold and the lust to build one web upon another, I looked for love in all the wrong places. Seeking for that kind of love one can get from a man, and I made poor decisions. My family member molested me and did not love me, nobody loves me, and everybody hates me kept ringing in my mind and ears. I knew my mom's love is unconditional, and yet I wanted a man's love. My dad did not love me, so I thought. Here are two men in my life who should have loved me and yet did not. So, I began the quest to find a man's kind of love. I soon found myself in a relationship with a man (or young boy, some might say), and at seventeen, lust certainly showed up for me and apparently others. Then to my surprise, I went to the bathroom at my house, and my boyfriend was in the bathroom with my babysitter having sex. Yet another reinforcement was that I was not good enough for men, and obvious disappointment swelled up within me. More to this story a bit later.

At nineteen, I fell in love, both with a man and with God. I accepted Jesus into my life, and an amazing lady prayed with me. I felt as though a thousand pounds lifted from my body. I married at twenty-one. I thought I was so in love. We had a good time going to parties, playing games, drinking, and hanging out with friends. Slowly as I got older, I realized there is more to life than the party scene, and I began to search for something more and seek God. My husband did not see it that way. One beer led to another, more and more often. I guess I did not notice the excessive drinking when I was younger and wanted to party myself. Then suddenly, I saw his inability to stop drinking and was completely scared. The numerous memories of my dad came crashing in. By now, I was not even speaking with my father, and here I was, reliving my childhood in my marriage. How could this happen? What in the world have I done? The very thing I despised; I was in the middle of. One time, I was begging him not to drink, and I saw violence with him slamming me into the closet door and punching it. It was almost as if I saw my mom's face at that very moment, and then strength began to arise in me. I let him know if he so much as laid a hand on me, I would not stay in the marriage. He stopped suddenly, and I left for a drive. That young girl once again arose and felt disappointment. Would yet another man in my life disappoint me? How come I am not good enough for men? Is there something wrong with me? With the closet incident, that night was yet another moment I shoved hurt and disappointment into the recesses of my heart and continued to build another fence around my heart. I knew when you got married, you were supposed to stick with it.

Divorce at that point was not an option for me. I did not want to disappoint my mom, God, and anyone else in my life, for that matter. I needed to be a good example and not disappoint others. As the years passed, my husband continued to drink and at levels that sometimes affected his functionality at work. I was so stressed my hair began to fall out. In clumps, I would lose hair, and I was very sick. I did not eat healthy foods. My day consisted of diet Coke and Mentos. Not the healthiest diet, I might add. I ended up in a size zero. Not going to lie; after two children, I would welcome a smaller size today. However, at that time in my life, I was not healthy physically, spiritually, and mentally. I went to tell my mom and stepdad that weekend that I could not do it anymore. I was emotionally and physically drained, and the marriage was not good for my health. As always, my mom, in her unconditional love, supported me. Looking back, I can see she had dealt with the same type of pain and disappointment in life, and she got me, she understood me. I returned from my mom's, and on the three-hour drive full of stress, replayed the words over and over in my head of what I would say to my husband, fearing how he would react.

Would he act out? Would he tell me how I was not good enough for him? God, in his mercy, did the work for me. When I walked into a dark house, lights out, and no car in the driveway, I made my way into the kitchen and found my "Dear John" letter. I never thought getting a letter like that would be ultimately freeing, and yet it was. I was free in my mind. In the days ahead, I would find pornography and drugs in my home. I began to understand the heaviness and stress I was feeling. I immediately filed for divorce after nearly eleven years of marriage. *What's Lust Got To Do With It?* Everything!

In the most unsuspecting time of my life, when I was not looking, I found true love. The love of my life showed up in the most unconventional way. Love from someone who did not care about the baggage I brought and loves me for me. Yes, just as I was – damaged, hurt, and with all my poor decisions, he loved me for me. The first man who portrayed the unconditional love that one would get from a father. The funny thing is he did not even know God, and yet he was so hungry to learn of the God I serve, the God who brought me through all the hurt, loved me despite my poor decisions, and has open arms for all those who choose to serve him. This person, after almost two years of dating, became my husband. He has loved me through all the trials too. When you come into a relationship with all the hurt and trials of the past, let me tell you, the relationship is not all roses. For years, he was constantly having to tell me he loves me the way I am, tells me I am good enough, and I do not have to explain my every step. He trusts me and loves me.

When a person has been hurt and disappointed, it is hard to believe trust and love truly exist. Yet it does! Both from the Father in heaven and also someone on earth who will be a vessel of God to show you unconditional love. I am blessed to have that example from my mom, husband, and now children and grandchildren. I am thankful that one night on the bridge, there was a *yes* to God and *no* to jumping. I sit here writing this excerpt of Mom's book with four generations of love and blessings.

Well, now it is time to finish some of the untold stories and share how to overcome during turmoil. I was sitting at a conference, which was delivered by a dear friend of mine. The conference was on the topic, "That's Your Story?" As my friend was discussing the spiritual root of disease and illness and characteristics of behavior, I had a boulder come down and smack me in the face. If you want a visual, imagine the song *"Wrecking Ball"* (Miley Cyrus) and that huge wrecking ball coming down and smacking me right in the face. My friend began to give the characteristics of unforgiveness, and I realized the web of lust, hurt, and unforgiveness had created a root of bitterness in my life I had not let go of. So began the journey of restoration, which I might add is a daily journey. In the last five years, I have let go of so many things. Every day I feel a piece of freedom being given back. To experience forgiveness, however, does require action.

I first began praying for those who hurt me, wishing the best blessing for them and their life. I realized through those prayers that the unforgiveness ran deep into the recesses of my heart. God even gave me a visual of veins with the unforgiveness running through the blood of my veins, and it had to be cut out and released. I realized I truly forgave the family member who had molested me. There was only one thing left to do, tackle the unforgiveness I was hanging onto with my dad, or so I thought. I had not talked to my dad in fifteen years. I kept telling myself that I was protecting others from the disappointment I experienced when really, I was holding onto unforgiveness. It took me a while to build up the courage to make the call. I mustered up all the courage I had and punched in his number on my cell. I started the conversation, "Dad, it's me, Vickie; I am so sorry I have not called you in so long." He said, "It is ok, honey; I knew you were probably really busy." I thought to myself and almost chuckled – really? busy? for fifteen years. I proceeded to ask for forgiveness, and as I did, he asked for forgiveness and started apologizing for not being there, and for missing out on the important milestones in my life. I asked if we could meet so he could meet my husband and children. He said yes, and the path of forgiveness began. Shortly after, he had a stroke which he survived. I was so thankful for God's mercy. Had I not started the path of forgiveness; I would have stressed myself out with blame. God's timing is perfect.

My step forward started the forgiveness journey for my brother and sister too. They had not spoken to him in years, and he had not talked to them either or met their children. I am not suggesting putting yourself in unsafe situations; however, there are many ways to begin the forgiveness journey. For me, it was the reconnection. I started the path without expecting anything in return. I knew God would use my step of faith as a diving board to healing. I did not realize that His grace abounds so much that He used it as a healing for my siblings, too. It probably even brought some healing to my mom as well.

That journey continues. I do not have the same relationship as a little girl who grows up with her daddy; however, I can say I love my dad and will honor him for the rest of my life. You see, he also was a party to the lust web in his life. He also experienced hurt as a child with rejection and disappointment. This in no way excuses poor behavior; however, it does help us to realize we are all on a journey. If we can extend just a little bit of the mercy our King gives us, we can walk through the journey, and that makes our steps go towards Him, and He is with us on the journey.

As I continued to walk out of the unforgiveness into forgiveness, I opened Pandora's box. I have now realized I had to settle the score of unforgiveness with my ex-husband. I talked to my amazing husband and explained what I felt I needed to do, and he immediately gave me permission to make the call. I sent a private message and asked to talk. He said yes. He has since remarried as well. I began to tell him I was sorry I had held unforgiveness to him, and I am who I am today through the experiences in our marriage. I asked for forgiveness for holding things against him. He began to do the same. We spoke for about thirty minutes, thanked each other for the experiences we shared, and asked for forgiveness where we may have hurt each other. Another piece of the walls around my heart is healed. You see, one of the things I had to do was look at the things myself.

I had a deep dark secret I had shared with no one except my mom. How would I ever let go of this secret? How would I ever forgive myself? In all the journey to forgiveness, I somehow thought I could overcome all without forgiving myself. Remember my story of looking for love in all the wrong places? The story of being seventeen and my boyfriend caught in the sexual act with my babysitter. Well, there is more to the story. I was pregnant. I wish I could say I was as brave and courageous as my mom was that night on the bridge. I wish I could tell you that piece of the story had a happy ending. Oh, I so wish I had made a different choice. Boy, am I glad for God's mercy. At almost eighteen, this broken, damaged little girl did the very thing she despised and made a disappointing decision I live with today. I had an abortion. I did not save my little baby as my mom did hers. The regret I lived with for thirty-three years before allowing God to help me let go at times was unbearable. *What's Lust Got To Do With It* is definitely an understatement.

I began the journey of forgiving myself; I first told my husband. We both believe abortion is not an option and not a decision a woman should make. For him, it is his belief; for me, it is the agony of 33 years of unforgiveness for myself and regret. I would even go as far as to say moments of hating myself. I cannot change it; I cannot have a redo; it is. Not a day goes by that I do not think of that decision, my baby, what I did, and how I made a poor decision. I feel that I really did not understand the decision I made. In 1983, abortion was thought to be accepted. Many articles said the baby was not formed. With the technology we have access to now and my walk with the Lord today, I know that is not true. With my story if I can save one life from being aborted or help even one person who is locked in the prison of secrecy and living with the hurt, regret, and unforgiveness of themselves, it is not for nothing.

My husband was amazing. He held me as I cried. Remember, I had only told my mom and never spoke of it again for thirty-three years. After my husband, my next conversation needed to be with my girls, the same girls who knew their mom's opinion of abortion and believed the same. It was as if I felt like a fraud heading into a talk with my daughters, who then were teenagers. Their love and mercy were unfathomable. Both of them had almost the same response. They said Mom, you can use your story to help others whom you may not be able to help had you not gone through that. Now I am in no way advocating abortion, however, God will use our faults and mistakes to help others overcome. They gave me a hug and said they wanted to be there when I shared my testimony. Well, as God would have it, that opportunity would come with a conference called "The Journey," where I was a speaker.

For the first time publicly, I shared my story. Of course, our heavenly Father sent women who needed to hear the story: women who had kept the secret, women who needed to let it go and receive the healing our King offers.

If life were a puzzle, you can see how, in fact, these pieces all fit together. The lust and generational curses can weave a web you are unaware of at times. We all have a journey we are traveling. God is there to extend His mercy and grace. He forgives us and unconditionally loves us. You can be encouraged that no matter what experiences are in your life, God wants us to walk in His joy, in His presence, and His guidance will provide us the way:

> Therefore, there is now no condemnation for those who are in Christ Jesus, because through Christ Jesus the law of the Spirit who gives life has set you free from the law of sin and death. For what the law was powerless to do because it was weakened by the flesh, God did by sending his own Son in the likeness of sinful flesh to be a sin offering. And so, he condemned sin in the flesh.
>
> –Romans 8:1-3, NIV

We are free, free indeed in Him.

Examine yourself for any unforgiveness you may be holding on to and determine your emotions around it. Then pray for those for whom you have unforgiveness. Praying for the best for them and asking God to bless them. Then when circumstances permit, go to the person, or if it is not safe, write the person (even if you do not send the letter). Remember to lay pride and anger aside and approach with His mantle upon you. The Father can help you with this, and He will. Seek the Word of God and develop your relationship with the Father. Ask him to show you what you can learn from the situation or circumstance.

Sometimes you may need a visual: cancel the debt of unforgiveness, write the hurt on a piece of paper, crumble it and throw it away or burn it, and write a blank check of forgiveness. Remember not to allow gossip to creep in; instead, ask God to show you another perspective. Do seek out a mentor, a coach, or someone who will encourage you to seek the Father and let go of those things that bind you. In the end, you must make a commitment to forgive. Is it hard? Yes. Will it attempt to creep back in? Yes. Remember, since before the earth was formed, our Father has great plans for you and your life. Your situation may give hope to the 4th generation and beyond.

In my story, the last five years, I look back and know that God has used my story to help others and has brought joy back into my life. I am full of gratitude. Each day is a walk on the journey; I still experience rocks and sometimes boulders. Yet in Him, it is well with my soul. Is it well with you, too?

THE 7 STEPS TO BREAKING THE BONDAGE OF YOUR PAST

7 Steps

Healing Proceeds Liberty

Have you ever felt wounded – mentally, physically, and/or spiritually? The good news is that God has a plan for our lives and has called us out of darkness into the freedom and liberty we deserve. Even though we may know we are called to live in Joy, sometimes those words seem so far in the distance that we do not know how to begin a journey toward the liberty and healing we seek. There is Good News! No matter your experiences, hurts, and disappointments, there are steps you can take. Seven steps that, when we identify and apply them to our lives, can take us on this journey.

As with any journey, pebbles and even boulders may be on the road; however, knowing the path is truly half the battle. Take each of these steps at your own pace. If you get stuck, go on to the next step and come back to this step later. This chapter is your workbook to make this healing your reality. Before you start, list the What's and the Whys.

What is it you want? List these what's. Freedom from anxiety and depression? To live a rich, full life? Only you know the what's. Then, make a list of the whys. I am doing this so my children will be free from my mistakes. I never want to make the same mistakes again. I want to get married again and be free from my past. Only you know the whys. Make a thorough list. You will never follow through if you don't know what you want to accomplish and why. You must decide before we start. Remember, in Chapter 9, I had to decide or lose myself. Now you must decide, too. The decision is to find your true self.

These are the steps I used, and I continue to use them when I find that the past is interfering with the present. These steps are often ongoing and, in some sense, never-ending. Sometimes, when I get stuck, I can go back through the process and discover something I missed or gain a new insight into my life. Here are all the steps. As you read on, you will find these Steps can be a path toward a new freedom in your life:

Step 1: Realize the Need to Change YOUR LIFE

Step 2: No Event Defines Who You Are

Step 3: Forgive Yourself.

Step 4: Forgive, for Your Sake, Not Those Who Hurt You

Step 5: Letting Go of What Happened

Step 6: Lessons Learned From the Pain

Step 7: Gratitude is Possible

Step 1: Realize the Need to Change Your LIFE

Seek God's direction: This is the first step on this journey to healing and liberty. I realized I needed to heal and surrender to HIS process for my healing. I realized that the circumstances, harm and hurt, do not define us. They are just a piece of our lives, a snapshot in time. We do not need to add to the story unforgiveness, anger, bitterness, and any other emotion because of bad experiences in our lives.

So, I acknowledge the event that happened and that I need to heal. But that it is just an event that happened. Know that it is not who you are, and God has greater things. I heard God had something better for my life when I stepped off that bridge and chose life. The molestation of my uncle never defined me. It affected me. But it was an event that I dealt with. The same is true for you. I had no idea that the event was generational and was not personal. Might yours be the same? Often, we can create additional stories around what happened, we get to write the next chapter in our story, and we can choose to start from a fresh canvas:

> When you pass through the waters, I will be with you; and when you pass through the rivers, they will not sweep over you. When you walk through the fire, you will not be burned; the flames will not set you ablaze.
>
> –Isaiah 43:2, NKJV

Tell God, I am surrendering all the circumstances and stories I have told myself to you, Lord. I surrender to you and your process for healing me. Make a list of any obstacles that stand in the way of your healing and how you will overcome them.

Remember to begin your meditations by combatting some of the doubts you may have about your life and limits you may have imposed on yourself. Psalm 138:8, CSB, says: "The Lord will fulfill His purpose for me. Lord, your faithful love endures forever."

Ask God to fulfill the purpose in your life. Surrender not my will Lord but yours be done. It sounds easy, right? Yet, it may not be as easy as it sounds. To surrender our will to God's will is a little scary for those who have experienced trauma. We may find it hard to trust God or anyone. Intellectually, we may know God is good, wise, and loving. But the problem is not what we know about God; instead, this problem is about our automatic emotional reaction based upon our painful experience of when our trust was betrayed. We find ourselves being guarded, never wanting to be disappointed or hurt again. I have used trust issues as an example of a common problem that hangs on when lust has led to emotional injury. While there are other problems stemming from trauma, the important point is first to identify and define those problems that most interfere with our recovery. What are some other areas you struggle in? Do you find it hard to set limits or stay calm in stressful situations? Do you panic when others are in control? Does simple embarrassment lead you to shame? Do you feel guilty without knowing why? Sometimes fearful for no reason? These are typical trauma responses. Remember through the process to put these issues into God's loving hands. Remember, HE is guiding the process. Don't try to take back control. "He heals the brokenhearted and bandages their wounds" (Psalm 147:3, CSB).

Journal, Journal, Journal! This will be key. To get it all out in the open for you to examine it for what it is. Write about what happened to you. Make the connections to the trauma responses we just talked about. Who did it to you and acknowledge how it made you feel. It is okay to acknowledge the pain and how it hurt you. Then acknowledge it was not your fault. You didn't want it to happen. It was an event that occurred. This step is often very difficult. It could take hours, days, or weeks. Do not rush the process. Find a quiet place to write and then absorb and understand what you wrote. You may have stuffed the pain and emotion for years. Now is the time to acknowledge the pain, grieve it, and examine it for what it really is. It is okay to grieve the innocence lost, etc.

Trauma responses are automatic. Now is your chance to understand them and heal. To rewire your brain so they are no longer automatic. In all your steps of healing, remember how a physical injury heals – a scab forms to protect the wound from reinjury. If you pull the scab off too soon, it leaves a scar. The Lord designed your skin, so the scab falls off at just the right time, leaving the skin beneath new, soft, and nice. I am trusting that if you choose to read this book, you are at the healing stage of your emotional injury. Your emotional healing mirrors physical healing. There may have been a crusty hardness that protected your sensitivity for a season. Changes are occurring, and the time is coming in your emotional life when the hardness falls away, and a newness will shine through.

Journal Insights

Journal Insights

Journal Insights

Step 2: **No Event Defines Who You Are**

If you have done this, then it is time to Stop! Defining who you are is God's job. Now, let's take another step towards liberty and healing by erasing some lies and distortions. It is time to realize that events and hurts do not define us. These are small pieces of our lives among the myriad of things we have experienced. Yet, memories of traumatic events have grown enormously in our minds by the emotional impact of the insults we have attached to the events. The work of this step is to clear our names and let God tell us who we are.

The Psalmist reminds us in Psalm 139 (CBS) that God's thoughts of us are more than the total grains of sand on the seashore. How precious we are to HIM. So, while we acknowledge the events that happened, we do not give them the power to hang a label on us because God's thoughts about us trump any other thoughts. Likely, what you have been saying to yourself about the event or what others have said is not true or is only partially true. A very young child who is brutally beaten may believe they deserve those blows. Is that true? Of course not. Is the young victim of molestation at fault because the perpetrator said they were irresistible? Never! These events are the facts of what happened to us. We must stick to the facts and drop the perpetrator's excuses, the labels others may give us, and the names we call ourselves. Know that your connection to the event is not who you are. Remember, when I stepped off the bridge, I heard God say that HE had something much better for my life. So, in God's vision of who I am, the molestation by my uncle never defined me. Now, I can completely agree with God's vision of who I am because he has enabled me to trust what HIS Word says about who I am in Jesus, my Messiah. This can be for you, too.

Further, I had no idea this event was a generational family pattern. The last chapter, by my daughter Vickie, identified some of those generational issues. Her account added another layer to my mother's experience and mine.

However, we get to write the next chapter. God provides us with a fresh start, the blank page to a new journal. We get to begin a new chapter in our journey. Be sure to journal. Nothing will help you clarify your thoughts and sort out your emotions like journaling. Write about what happened to you. Who did it to you? Acknowledge the pain and the way you feel about what happened. Yell about it, cry about it. Whatever you need to do to empty yourself of the experience. You more than likely have stuffed those feelings or have not allowed yourself to get it all out. But your body remembers. That is why you sometimes have emotions that seemingly come from nowhere. Unload the pain now. Allow yourself to empty yourself. Did you ever wonder why you feel so good after a good cry? It is because it is cleaning to release those pent-up emotions.

Journal Insights

Journal Insights

Journal Insights

Step 3: Forgive Yourself

Does it seem odd to you that in a book designed to address how lust can lead to situations where people are victimized, that a whole step toward recovery was devoted to forgiving yourself? Hey! I am the victim here. What did I do that needs forgiving? While what happened to us wasn't a poor or bad decision on our part, we still blame ourselves. This response is especially true in trauma situations such as molestation, rape, or physical abuse just to name a few. You may not even know that you have unforgiveness with yourself. This self-loathing may show up in many forms. Do you find it difficult to accept compliments? Do you keep finding yourself in the same situations with hurtful relationships? This list is not all-inclusive; however, anger, eating disorders, and physical harm to yourself are all signs of self-unforgiveness. How do you forgive yourself?

Yet even though we were blameless in what happened to us, this is how many victims feel. We feel that we are shameful, dirty, and disgraced by what happened to us. These negative feelings were something I felt as the result of my own abuse, and I have counseled many women who felt this same sense of shame, as if there was something tainted about us.

This is usually the result of the excuses from the perpetrator. These are attempts to put onto us what belongs to them. Yet feeling shame is not about something you did wrong. We have all known of people who felt shame about coming from a poor family, about our appearance, or a family member who went to prison. Do you see what all these circumstances have in common? Each of these people were feeling shame about something they could not control.

So, shame usually is not related to something we did wrong, but instead, it is feeling not as good as other people. Which, of course, has no basis for us to feel shame. So, if you have assigned any shame to yourself because of your abuse, then it is time to re-think this idea. The abuse did not touch your value. You are just as priceless as if this never happened to you. Prayer, repeating scriptures on who we are in Him, and daily affirmations are all ways to forgive ourselves and self-acceptance. I want you even to go as far as to speak out loud: *God forgave me, and I forgive myself. There is nothing I can do or say that God has not already forgiven me for.* Place this statement everywhere so that you can see it and let it penetrate your soul. You are His masterpiece, and God does not make mistakes.

This step may be a long part of the journey. You can continue in each step while you are walking out the other steps. Forgiving yourself is one that likes to creep back in. Remember, it is finished; you are forgiven. Remind yourself of this often, and it will give you strength.

The guilt you have felt, or the shame, was never yours to begin with. It belonged to the perpetrator, not to you. We often tell ourselves that there must be something wrong with us. Every time I have a relationship failure, I ask myself, "What is wrong with me?" Something must be wrong with me, or else it would not keep happening to me. We forget that we are responding to the trauma event that has already happened rather than the current situation. This is why we must forgive ourselves for whatever happened to us. "There is therefore now no condemnation for those who are in Christ Jesus" (Romans 8:1, CSB).

I suggest to you something that may sound strange to you, but it works. Suppose you were a child when you were violated. Put a picture of yourself at 4 or 5 years old on a bathroom mirror or someplace where you will see it daily. Look at yourself and repeat over and over at least twice a day, on rising and before you go to bed:

You are a beautiful child. It is not your fault. What happened in your childhood is not your fault. You are an amazing child. You are smart. You are talented; there is nothing you cannot do. God designed you to be powerful, and you are designed for greatness and success. You can do all things through Christ who strengthens you!

Keep repeating all these positive affirmations daily. Add even more affirmations as they come to mind. What was it your child-self needed to hear from your parent that you never heard? I am asking you now to reparent yourself. It is still possible; you are not too old to be reparented. You can parent yourself to self-love and confidence. Freedom from the shame and guilt that never belonged to you in the first place is just around the corner. You have carried it unjustly for those who hurt you.

If you were an adult when the violation occurred, remind yourself the same. You are the daughter of the King of the Universe and are in no way to blame yourself for what happened to you. Now is the time to dump the load. You will continue this exercise throughout your journey until you don't need it anymore.

Journal Insights

Journal Insights

Journal Insights

Step 4: Forgive, for Your Sake, Not Those Who Hurt You

The Fourth Step on your journey is to forgive those who have hurt you. Forgive for your sake and benefit, not theirs. Forgive how they hurt you spiritually, psychologically, and physically. This Step may be one of the most important steps for you to complete. It is a difficult but necessary step.

Forgiveness does not mean you are saying what was done to you is okay. It simply means you will not allow it to take hold of your life. Forgiveness is not the absence of pain but the presence of mercy walking out forgiveness. You are going to forgive the other person so that you can release what is hurting you. It is weighing you down, not them. Sometimes, you think you have forgiven, but you have not.

Hidden unforgiveness is a real thing. It causes you to hang onto blame, insecurities, lack of trust, and many other attributes that impact relationships and daily life. Only after forgiveness can you truly move forward in liberty and healing. To begin this part of the journey, you must pray for the other person.

Pray the very best for the person and their life. These prayers can be challenging, yet know as you do this repeatedly, you will see a difference and feel the actual release in your heart. If the person is no longer alive, pray to the Father and ask that He bring healing and forgiveness to that situation. You should do this anyway. Another action you can take is to write a letter to the person. Even if you do not mail it, getting it down on paper can help you in the forgiveness journey. Calling the person is another action you can take if they are still alive. All the actions mentioned can bring you further on your path to forgiveness. "And be kind to one another, tenderhearted, forgiving one another, even as God in Christ forgave you" (Ephesians 4:32, NKJV). By forgiving them, you are being kind to yourself.

Forgiveness is not for the wrongdoer, the person who hurt you. It is for you. When we don't forgive, we are allowing that person who hurt us space in our heads and power in our lives. Why would you want to do that? They have already taken enough from you; why give them more?

Psalm 46:10, NKJV, says: "Be *Still* and know that I am God." In Hebrew, the word for "still" also means to let it go, to drop it. To know God is to be still. Let it go or drop it! That verse also says God will be exalted in the earth! Imagine that God is exalted by your ability to let it go and drop it.

Visualize a long, heavy rope. Now you are pulling that rope. Everyone who has ever hurt you is hanging onto that rope like in a tug-a-war game. Your parents, boyfriends, girlfriends, husbands, wives, business partners, pastors, and friends. You must name and list those who are hanging on. Imagine pulling all of them through your life and into all your relationships. No wonder life feels so weary and relationships so difficult. Look at everyone who is involved. Now, visualize dropping the rope. Turn around and notice all of those you have let go of. Now, walk away free! You are no longer dragging these people into all your relationships and your life.

Until you forgive them and let them go, that is what you are doing. Look how many you invite into your life, marriage, relationships, or even your children's lives. Is it time to pull their power plug?

Remember that forgiveness does not mean you will renew your relationship with the person who betrayed you, and they will have your trust. It means that you will no longer allow them power in your life. It also does not mean you will have amnesia and forget what they have done. It just means you have taken the sting out of what they did. You will lose the anger and the bitterness that only hurts you. They can no longer affect your life, decisions, or happiness. You have taken their power away. Freedom!

Journal Insights

Journal Insights

Journal Insights

Step 5: Letting Go of What Happened

The Fifth Step on the journey is to let it go. Now, this is arguably one of the hardest to do. It sounds so easy, though, doesn't it? To let it go, you must admit you are hanging onto it. *Just let it go.* If it were that easy, everyone would do that. A big piece of this step is predicated on Step Four. The more we walk in the forgiveness of others, the more we can let go. Write down the things you are holding onto, even if it is anger, unforgiveness, or emotions that have negatively impacted your life and relationships. Write down situations that have caused you to be bitter. Meditate on it. Recognize it, acknowledge it, or admit it. Then, wad the paper up and throw it away or burn it. Say "It is finished!" out loud as you are doing it. I know this sounds silly, but it works! Repeat as often as necessary. God will expose new things to you that you need to let go of.

Yes, it is a journey, and believe it or not, as you get rid of one stronghold and feel freedom and liberty, God may reveal another. For some of us, we have built layers and fences in the recesses of our hearts. You may have pushed them so deep that you do not even realize they are there. I know I certainly did. The freedom you feel each time is worth the journey. "Do not be anxious about anything, but in every situation, by prayer and petition with thanksgiving, present your requests to God" (Philippians 4:6, NKJV).

I once went on an extended fast. After my divorce, I went to a cabin to spend two weeks in total solitude. I only took a Bible, a journal, a pen, and clothes with me. There was no Internet, WIFI, or phone – just me and God. I spent hour upon hour in prayer and meditating and writing.

One night, I found myself on the floor crying like a baby, screaming Daddy, why did you leave? Why did you leave me? I felt something like a deep root being ripped out of my soul. It was physically painful. If you told me two weeks earlier that I had unforgiveness towards my dad, I would have said, "You are crazy." There is no way that could be true. I loved my dad! He was my anchor! I am telling you this so you realize how deeply things may be buried and that you may need to let go of them. Some things that, like me, you are perhaps unaware of.

That is why you must take time with each step. You must trust the process. Don't try and rush it. We all want things done in microwave time. But some things must be done in a slow cooker fashion because we have spent years stuffing and hiding feelings until they are deeply buried.

I know you can do this. Because I did, and I have helped hundreds of others do the same. You are a warrior, a champion. Conquer your fear, and you will win your freedom.

Seek God; He will guide you. We need guidance and direction. There will be times when you do not know what to do next. He does. When relationships on earth fail us, His love is unconditional and perfect. Build your relationship with our King and Lord. He will see you through and give you hope and encouragement along the way:

> The LORD will guide you continually, and satisfy your soul in drought, and strengthen your bones; You shall be like a watered garden, and like a spring of water, whose waters do not fail.
>
> —Isaiah 58:11, NKJV

By surrendering to the Lord, you are giving Him the power to move in your life to guide, direct, and lead you into all truth. Lord, not my will but yours be done. Sounds easy, but it, too, is a matter of trust. Can we trust Him with our hearts and our lives? We all have trust issues to one degree or another. But He is worthy of your trust. Remember – All things are working together for our Good to those who love Him.

He has a process, too. He made us. He understands how our brains work and how our trauma has worked against us in the fulfillment of our lives and the fulfillment of who He created us to be. He also knows how our brain has helped us to survive by hiding memories we were not yet ready to process. Let Him guide you in all these steps.

Remember how physical injuries work. You develop a scab to protect the wound from reinjury, giving it a chance to heal. If you pull the scab off too soon, it leaves a scar. The Lord knows exactly when to remove the scab so that the skin underneath is nice and new. This is how He is healing our emotional issues. That crust hardness kept us from getting hurt for a season, but if you are reading this, I believe He is saying now is the time to let your newness shine through.

Journal Insights

Journal Insights

Journal Insights

Step 6: Lessons Learned From the Pain

What did I or can I learn from what happened to me? God is always in the process of bringing redemption to our stories. What happened to me was not the path I would have chosen for myself, but it has made me a more compassionate and understanding person.

I have helped countless victims of sexual and physical abuse turn their pain into gain and power. Through the pain of my divorce, I have helped others come out of feeling rejected and become useful and powerful champions. What can we learn from the situations we are in?

Often, if we focus on what we have learned, the pain can diminish because we are moving forward. Learn what forgiveness means to you. Maybe you previously thought that forgiveness is more for the benefit of the person who wronged you than yours. Once the relationship is on the path to restoration, and you've given yourself time to accept the reality of the past, it will be clear that forgiveness is a way for you to find closure. Closure means something bringing healing and liberty: "I instruct you in the way of wisdom and lead you along straight paths" (Proverbs 4:11, NKJV).

It is also time to reflect. How has God turned your pain into your power? Write down all the pain, the rejection, the betrayal. Now, reflect on how God has used those things to make you a better parent. A better wife or husband? A better congregation leader? A better business leader? You fill in the blanks. More compassionate? More discerning? How are you now using these gifts to help others? Make a list of all the people you have helped through their difficulties.

Notice how your pain has been your gain in your life and the lives of others.

Journal Insights

Journal Insights

Journal Insights

Step 7: Gratitude is Possible

Practice this step-in-step with all the others. Focusing on gratitude tends to melt away your hurt and allows you to focus on the blessings of life. That will spill over into helping others in their lives. Gratitude creates contagious joy.

Every day, find 3-5 things you are grateful for. Be specific; no generalizing. For example, of course, you might be grateful for God and all HE has done for you, how He has rescued you again and again. Be grateful for your health, family, friends, and being alive. Be specific. It might sound like this: I am grateful for life because I can see the beauty outside, hear the birds chirping, and use my ability to help someone today.

Another example might be that I am grateful for my mom because yesterday, she called and said she was proud of me. I might be thankful for my dad and what a great example he has been. I am grateful for my children and how God has blessed me with them. I am blessed by my friends and how they have encouraged me. I thank God for my house and how He has supplied all of my needs. I can even be grateful for my community and how we worship together. There is no end to all we can be grateful for.

When you are specific, it is more meaningful and has a greater impact. Each day, at least one of your gratitude's should be a person or persons. Call or visit them and tell them how grateful you are for them. Be specific in telling them why you are grateful. You may be the very piece of encouragement they need. "Be thankful in all circumstances, for this is God's will for you who belong to Christ Jesus" (I Thessalonians 5:8, NKJV).

Even our trials are to be counted as joy. What? Yes, our trials, no matter what they are:

> Consider it pure joy, my brothers, and sisters, whenever you face trials of many kinds because you know that the testing of your faith produces perseverance. Let perseverance finish its work so that you may be mature and complete, not lacking anything.
>
> –James 1:2-4, NKJV

The good news is that no matter how difficult these steps are, God is always with us. We are on this journey called life. The path is sometimes rocky and hurtful, yet our God is here to restore us, redeem us, and bring joy, hope, and encouragement. He goes before us, and HE is with us and makes our paths straight:

> And the LORD, He is the One who goes before you. He will be with you; He will not leave or forsake you; do not fear or be dismayed.
>
> –Deuteronomy 31:8, NKJV

Fear and mistrust often hold us back from stepping out into our relationship with Jesus.

A relationship is the first step towards trust:

> Trust in the LORD with all your heart and lean not on your own understanding: In all your ways acknowledge HIM, And He shall direct your paths. Do not be wise in your own eyes; Fear the LORD and depart from evil. It will be health to your flesh and strength to your bones.
>
> –Proverbs 3:5-8, NKJV

When we lean upon our own understanding, we will do the same things we have always done. Our own ways are not healing or fruitful. They will generally keep us in bondage. Jesus came to set the captives free!

Remember, repetition by practicing these steps every day is very important. Practice will rewire your brain, and these practices will then become automatic to you. If you need help, by all means, please seek out a therapist or a coach who will keep you accountable. Will it be difficult? Yes! Will it be painful? Yes! However, the difficulty is a sign you are moving in the right direction. If it is not difficult, you are still in your comfort zone.

Nothing great ever happens in our comfort zones. Our progress and faith require us to move forward out of what we are comfortable with. Faith, by definition, according to the Book of Hebrews: "Now faith is the substance of things hoped for, the evidence of things not seen" (Hebrews 11:1, NKJV). So, of course, when we can't see something, there is a degree of discomfort and uncertainty. We all want instant comfort and results. We want microwave therapy. Truly rewiring our brain is likened to a process like a slow cooker, but how much sweeter is the taste? The fruit of our efforts will appear and is well worth the effort.

There is such freedom in becoming the person you were created to be. The empty feeling of never feeling good enough or not trusting anyone is over. If not now, when is the time? Go and be the champion you were destined to be. Take the first step today.

Journal Insights

Journal Insights

Journal Insights

www.ingramcontent.com/pod-product-compliance
Ingram Content Group UK Ltd.
Pitfield, Milton Keynes, MK11 3LW, UK
UKHW020244240426
12048UKWH00026B/1604